Illustration
FOR PROFIT

Illustration FOR PROFIT

A Manual for Success in Commercial Art

Bryan Foster

Long-eared owl (Asio otus)

BLANDFORD PRESS

LONDON · NEW YORK · SYDNEY

Dedicated to Daniel Pettiward whose conversation
with a friend prompted me to write this book

First published in the UK 1988 by Blandford Press,
an imprint of Cassell Plc
Artillery House, Artillery Row, London SW1P 1RT

Distributed in the United States by
Sterling Publishing Co., Inc.,
2 Park Avenue, New York, NY 10016

Distributed in Australia by
Capricorn Link (Australia) Pty Ltd
PO Box 665, Lane Cove, NSW 2066

British Library Cataloguing in Publication Data

Foster, Bryan
  Illustration for profit: a manual for success
  in commercial art.
  1. Commercial art
  I. Title
  741.6   NC997
ISBN 0 7137 1613 4

Typeset by Best-set Typesetter Ltd. Hong Kong
Printed in Spain by Graficas Reunidas, Madrid

CONTENTS

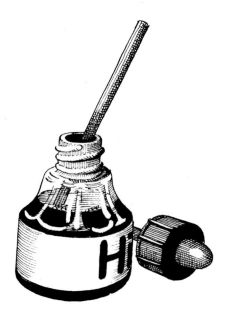

INTRODUCTION

As the title suggests, this book is intended for those who would like to learn a little more about the world of commercial art at a practical, everyday level. Therefore the aim is to introduce those interested in the subject to the practices and procedures of the commercial artist, thus making this an introduction to an introduction.

The fundamental difference between this book and others is in its undisguised and unashamed approach to art, based on the assumption that very few of us can afford to sit and paint or draw our time away with a total disregard for payment at the end of the day. A commercial artist has to be what his name implies, and to that end his approach must be coloured.

This book then will lay bare the methods and philosophy, the short cuts and grey areas, the pitfalls and snags, where other books deal in detail with the question of 'How To Draw' and 'How To Paint' with the emphasis on techniques accompanied by examples of the work of past masters in the field. Here I shall not be including the work of any past master for the very good reason that I believe the aim of the book can be best served by keeping it as the personal effort of an experienced commercial artist to pass on the tips and solutions he has acquired in his career.

The drawings and diagrams themselves are purposely drawn in various styles with a variety of pens and pencils, to add interest and consideration for the reader. There is a note accompanying each one describing the method. It will be noticed that the areas of work described and illustrated are very wide and it may be the basis for criticism that to work so widely inevitably means that perfection is not achieved in any particular field. It is nonetheless quite sensible because it more or less ensures a continuous flow of work from one direction or another and makes for a much more interesting life into the bargain.

It is only fair that I should point out to those about to embark on this sort of life that they must be prepared for a great deal more 'run-of-the-mill' everyday work than ever there will be of the exciting advertising campaigns and glossy holiday brochures – these come at odd intervals and provide the jam on the bread. Most of their time will be spent on the small jobs, uninteresting and downright boring jobs, sometimes taking no more than an hour or so to complete and certainly taking longer to get the materials out and then cleaned up afterwards than ever the job takes to do. And since we are concerned with making a living, these are the dangerous ones because they are so difficult to price.

I have included as many snippets of information as I can in the following pages, and although one picture is said to be worth a thousand words, sometimes the information cannot be transposed into pictorial form. With that in mind I should like to think that these pages had been read rather than looked at in order to derive the most benefit from them.

To earn a living in commercial art requires a certain attitude of mind; it is not the slightest bit of good setting out with purist views on how a watercolour must be done or how figures should be drawn. The only way to profit is the quickest and most effective at the time. I quote from a book on graphic art I was shown recently which said, 'The secret of graphic design is not to be afraid of cheating'. Well, I regret to say that is also very true throughout the whole of commercial art, not just graphic design. Therefore to be a success I suggest you remember that. After all, most of the world's greatest artists used some sort of aid or device to help them perfect their work ... why shouldn't you?

1 MATERIALS

As the world of commercial art is essentially a visual one, I cannot emphasise too strongly the necessity for using not only the correct materials but also the best, because in no other field more than art does it become so obvious if the wrong or poor materials are used. It will quickly become apparent in two ways; first by the artist or designer finding that they have difficulty in producing the finish they are looking for, or, even worse, finding it impossible to achieve the result they are seeking because of the materials they are using. It must therefore be recognised from the beginning that the right tools, materials and equipment are of paramount importance if professional work is to be the result ... and this book is all about the professional world of commercial art.

Papers

We can make a very good beginning with paper, as this is probably the most widely-used support (the name given to the material on which artists and designers do their work). Papers, then, can be conveniently divided into three types: hot-pressed, cold-pressed, and rough.

Hot-pressed paper has a hard smooth surface which is very suitable for drawing with pencil, pen and ink or even line and wash; but it is not generally used for pure watercolour or any other type of paint.

Cold-pressed paper, often referred to as 'Not' (because it is *not* hot-pressed), has a textured, semi-rough surface and is ideal for most kinds of work, and very good for most kinds of painting and some drawing. It is the most popular of the three types.

Rough paper has a pronounced tooth to its surface which makes it a delightful paper for the more accomplished worker, as by virtue of its texture it gives back something visual to the artist, providing he can control it effectively. This is the favourite paper of the watercolourists.

The weight of the paper must also be considered, as this is equally important. A paper that is too thin will cockle up as soon as paint or ink is applied and, no matter how talented the work is or how carefully it was done, it will be ruined and work will have to stop. The weight refers to one ream of paper (480 sheets), therefore a 70 lb (104 gsm) paper will have a much greater tendency to cockle than, for instance, a 140 lb (208 gsm) paper.

Paper and card come in all colours and qualities for all uses, as well as white. If you are not familiar with them, do tell suppliers what you want it for and they will be able to advise you.

This picture illustrates the 'tooth' or texture of a paper.

The remedy for this cockling is to stretch the paper before starting work on it. To do this, first thoroughly soak it by laying it in a bath of water or otherwise by gently spongeing it all over with plenty of water from a basin or tap. When you have made sure the paper is thoroughly wet, hold it up by one edge for a moment or two to let all the surplus water run off. Then you are ready to lay the paper in position on the drawing board, making sure there is at least 1 in (2.5 cm) of spare board showing all round. Take a strip of gummed tape and run it along one edge of the paper/board, thus fixing that edge all the way along – that is important. Now do the same with the other three edges. Finally put a drawing pin into each corner of the paper where the gummed tape crosses over; this is an added precaution as there is an enormous tension on the paper as it dries. This will now have to be left until it is quite dry, and should be left to dry out naturally.

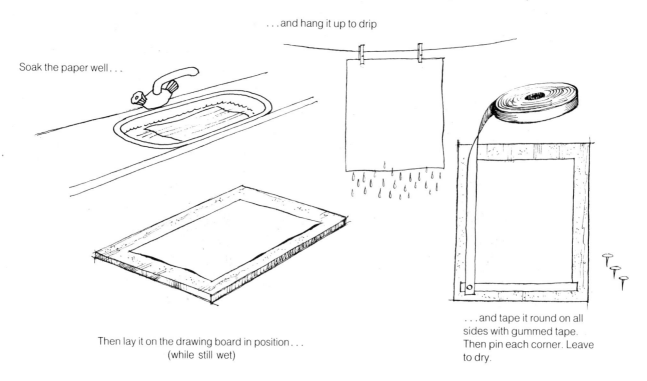

...and hang it up to drip

Soak the paper well...

Then lay it on the drawing board in position...
(while still wet)

...and tape it round on all sides with gummed tape. Then pin each corner. Leave to dry.

I must give a word of warning here. If the board on which the paper is being stretched is too thin or pliable, the shrinking paper may bend it up into a bow shape, leaving the paper like a drum skin. If this is likely to be the case it would pay to mount another piece of paper on the other side at the same time. The one will shrink against the other and the board will stay flat, resulting in both pieces of paper being usable.

Hand-Made Paper

As the name suggests, these papers are the very best and are a delight to handle and to work on. They are made with a very high linen-rag content and with very careful control over the impurity content of the product. There is a right and wrong side to these papers, the right side being coated with size, which makes it wonderfully receptive to watercolours of all types. As a matter of interest the right side of the paper can always easily be determined by viewing the water-mark the right way round.

Prepared Boards

This is a very convenient way to buy your paper, as it really is just thin paper mounted onto a board support. This, of course, does away with stretching and is much better for attaching overlays of all types, including protection covers.

Don't forget there is also a large range of coloured papers and boards available which can be very useful in creating just the right effect either at rough stage or at finished artwork.

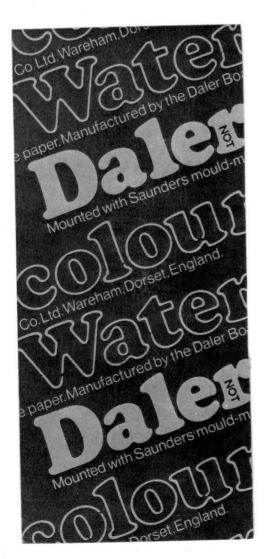

One of the advantages in using boards is that the type, quality and use are always printed on the back. This makes it easy to re-order.

Tracing Paper

Tracing paper is a product in a field all its own. A studio can be thrown into a state of chaos if they are not able to put a hand out and grab a piece of tracing paper. It can get you out of no end of trouble and often save the artist a great deal of time. I shall refer to it from time to time as the need occurs.

Drafting Film

This product is used in much the same way as tracing paper, with the added advantage that it is stable. Whereas tracing paper will cockle up if it is made wet with paint or ink, drafting film will not. Also it is not affected by changes in humidity and temperature, hence the term 'stable'. This makes it essential for overlays and register work. There are a number of drafting films on the market but the main difference between them is that some will take pencil and some will not, so be careful.

Masking Film

This is usually in the form of transparent self-adhesive plastic film which can be cut easily with a stencil knife to the various shapes needed, and then laid in position on the work. We shall return to this in detail in Chapter 10.

Masking film comes in roll form or flat sheet. Rolls are usually a bit more economical because you can cut off just exactly what you need, but sometimes the 'curling' can be a bit tiresome. I prefer sheets despite the wastage.

When preparing 'overlays' for register work, the film must be dimensionally stable – tracing paper *will not do*.

Masking Fluid

This is exactly as the name implies – masking that can be applied with a brush. It is a latex-based product which, when painted out with a brush, dries quickly to a thin rubbery film which can be peeled off by rubbing with a finger. It has a lot of uses, mainly where small intricate areas are to be masked.

Masking fluid can be used very successfully in conjunction with masking film and tape. Use it in the areas where it is difficult to cut the shape.

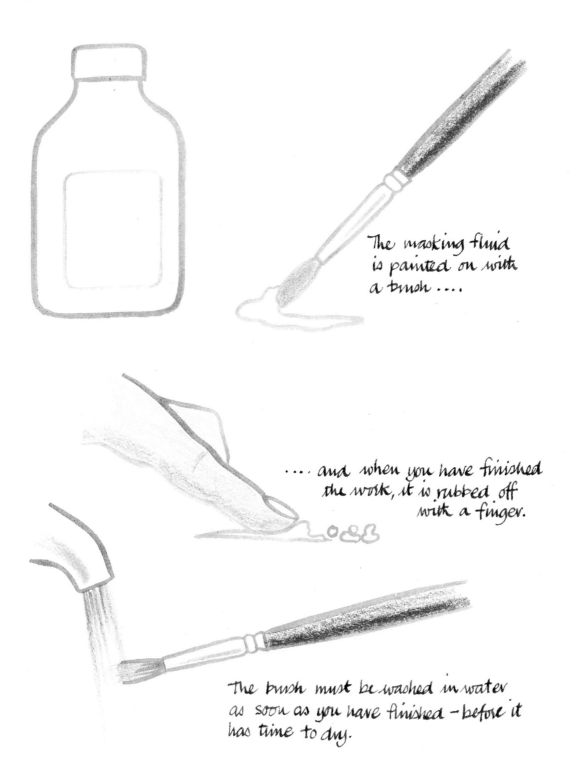

The masking fluid is painted on with a brush ....

.... and when you have finished the work, it is rubbed off with a finger.

The brush must be washed in water as soon as you have finished – before it has time to dry.

Spray Adhesive

This is an aerosol spray for mounting artwork or photographs. It is a wonderfully easy and safe way to achieve professional results. The job of mounting one's work has always been tiresome and yet so important. The alternative is to use double-sided tape. This has perhaps got wider applications than the aerosol in that it can successfully be used to fix notices to doors, posters to windows and letters to signs, and to fix together point-of-sale displays for stores and exhibitions.

Latex Adhesive

This is another latex-based product, available in tins and applied with a spatula, which serves a different function from the other two; its main use is for all the small-scale sticking jobs, such as pasting up material for magazines, books and newspapers. The great advantage of this type of adhesive is that, although it will hold permanently, it will also allow the joined pieces to be peeled apart, which is often essential, as frequently a certain amount of repositioning is called for during the make-up period.

There are not many spray adhesives on the market, so you don't have a lot of choice, whereas with double-sided tape there is a wide choice of type and width, so shop around.

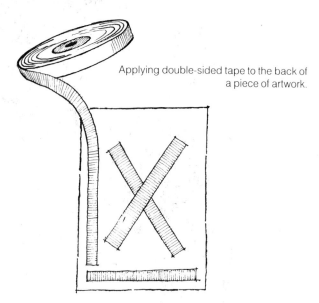

Applying double-sided tape to the back of a piece of artwork.

Try not to leave the lid off the Cow Gum any longer than is necessary: it will stay usable for years.

Inks

There is such a large selection of inks today, and because there is also an enormous selection of pens it is becoming very important to use the right ink with the right pen.

Largely they fall into two groups: the waterproof and the non-waterproof. The waterproof inks are used mainly with the ordinary steel dip pen, or otherwise with the stylo or technical pen, both of which are made specially to allow the rather heavy ink to flow without drying in the pen, which would clog it up and restrict the flow. There are now a few fountain pens that have been adapted to take these inks, and these are obviously very useful when the pen has to be used 'on site'. There is also a range of coloured waterproof inks which are used in exactly the same way as the blacks. The waterproof range is easily distinguishable as they dry with a fat glossy surface.

The non-waterproof inks, which can be used in any type of pen, are a little easier to use and can be thinned with distilled water to any consistency to give any intensity of colour. When applied to paper they sink in as they dry, leaving a matt surface.

The very shape of ink bottles will probably have some influence on your choice. The narrow neck bottles are very difficult and precarious to use. If you are using a dip-pen, it is always a good idea to tape the bottle down to the drawing board – it will save many a good drawing.

The church and the monk were drawn with a dip-pen using a fine nib.

Incidentally practically all the artwork in this book has been reduced from the original, but by various percentages.

Paints

Commercial colour work is done almost entirely with either watercolour, gouache, acrylic or oil colour. The choice of the type of colour used will depend on a number of considerations: for instance, whether the work is to be sited outside or inside; and whether it is for reproduction or just a single piece of artwork for use on its own. Also the style required by the customer will help determine the type of paint used.

The way to get the best out of watercolours is to leave the palette dirty. The mixing of fresh colour into old colours is a quick way to achieve all the subtle tones that make watercolour work so enchanting.

Although each type of paint has its own characteristics and properties which must be borne in mind before setting out on a job, the artist can also sometimes use one type of paint to better effect than another, and this too has to be considered carefully. For example, watercolour usually calls for a soft gentle approach to the subject, needing careful planning first and not allowing much in the way of alterations along the way, because the paint is transparent and so allows the first colour put down to show through the second and so on. Gouache, on the other hand, is opaque, and this allows one colour to be laid on top of another for ever and ever, each one covering the last without any trouble. This is one of the reasons why it is such a favourite among illustrators. The other main reason is because it reproduces so well. The colours have an even matt finish and are strong and permanent.

Often watercolour and gouache are used together, and these form a very successful combination. As they are both water-based and dry fairly quickly, the same mixing dishes can be used for both, as also can brushes, papers and sprays etc. Watercolour is bought in pans (which go into paint boxes) and gouache is bought either in tubes as designers' colour or in jars as poster colour.

A watercolour sketch of a local scene. The pencil outline drawing was done first and allowed to remain showing as part of the finished work. This is a method of 'line and wash' technique.

they set off through the wood........

This is a good example of the way in which gouache can be overpainted in any order, either light over dark or dark over light. You couldn't work this way in watercolour. It also shows the intensity of colour that is available with this type of paint, which is why it is such a favourite with commercial artists of all types.

This shows the way gouache is purchased. It is a very economical medium – the jars especially so if you keep them moist with water.

Acrylics

These are the newest colours to the range. One advantage of these paints is that they are waterproof when dry despite the fact that they are mixed, thinned and worked with water. These colours have good adhesion and can be used on metal, wood, concrete etc, which makes them very attractive for commercial work. Perhaps a small disadvantage is the speed with which the paint dries up in the brush, which must be kept softened all the time, and immediately it is finished with it must be thoroughly cleaned. Likewise the cap on the tube has a tendency to get clogged up and then dry, thus making it difficult if not impossible to get the cap back on, which in turn means that the whole tube dries up. The tip is to wipe round the neck of the tube with a damp cloth each time, which keeps it free of the paint which causes the trouble.

Acrylic tubes come in various sizes; do keep them rolled up from the bottom. If you have the type that don't want to stay rolled up – put a clothes peg on.

Oil Colour

Oils are synonymous with artists, of course, and they have their very obvious advantages. The one great difference to be remembered when using them is that they are best worked on a canvas arranged in a near vertical position. Therefore an easel of some sort has to be used and, although there are many sorts to choose from, the essential thing is that it accommodates the canvas, hardboard or wood panel on which you are going to work. One good method is to fix battens at a convenient height on the wall where the light is good, so that the artist can clamp his work to them. The advantage of this is that it keeps the floor space clear of easels, tables and lights, and makes good use of the walls which give a wonderfully firm support to the work with little danger of passing people brushing against wet work.

There is a wide range of mediums available to control the paint and to suit all types of approach, and the artist will have to establish what suits him best. As this book is not intended as a catalogue of materials I shall not attempt to list them here; they are well described in the books which are listed in the bibliography at the end.

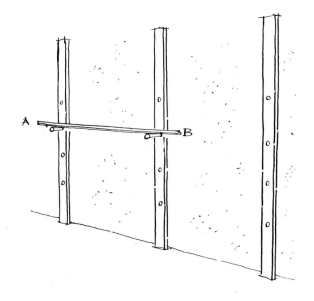

The batten AB can be moved up or down to suit the artist's comfort and makes it easier for working on large projects.

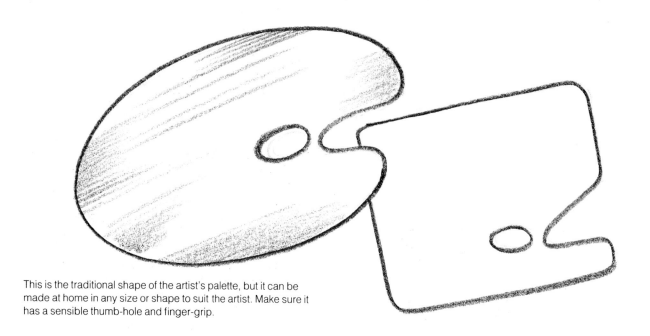

This is the traditional shape of the artist's palette, but it can be made at home in any size or shape to suit the artist. Make sure it has a sensible thumb-hole and finger-grip.

Masking Tapes

Masking tapes of all types are most useful and can help you get results that would be difficult to achieve in any other way. They come in varying widths and types. The most common is the paper masking tape which is ideal for masking up large areas of groundwork to be either painted or sprayed. This is also very useful for putting round the outside edge of any artwork at the commencement to ensure a nice sharp straight finish to the work.

There are also a number of low-tack cellulose tapes which give a razor-sharp edge to the paint, and these are most commonly used by signwriters to tape along the top and bottom edges of lines of lettering. It makes the lettering quicker to do and produces wonderfully straight lines of letters.

In this particular context it is of great importance to use a low-tack tape, otherwise there is a real danger of pulling off the ground colour when removing the tape; and if this happens to be on a brand new vehicle, for instance, it can turn out to have ruinous consequences.

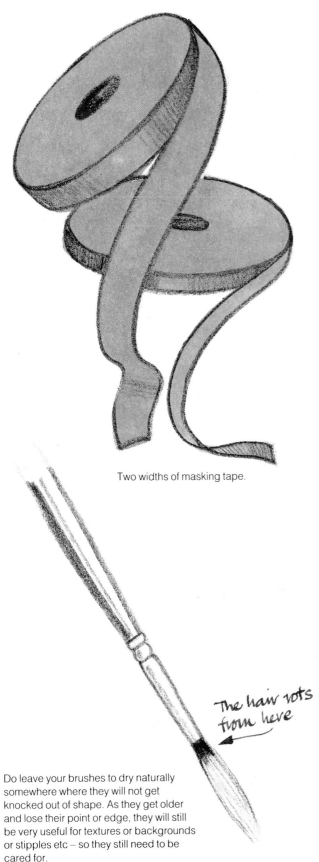

Two widths of masking tape.

The hair rots from here

Do leave your brushes to dry naturally somewhere where they will not get knocked out of shape. As they get older and lose their point or edge, they will still be very useful for textures or backgrounds or stipples etc – so they still need to be cared for.

Brushes

There are certain areas where the artist can save substantially on his outlay, for example by making his own easel, mahl stick or compasses, all with very successful results – but not so with brushes.

Brush-making is a highly-skilled trade, and therefore a good-quality one can and should cost more than a standard or student's quality product. As with paper, so with brushes; it is of the utmost importance always to buy the best you can afford. It is much better to have only a few different sizes and types, providing they are of good quality and in good condition.

Some artists are by nature rather untidy workers, and somewhat casual to say the least in their attention to maintenance. In the case of brushes this will reflect immediately in the work, either by making it slower to do or by quality in the finished piece. Therefore they must be cleaned thoroughly each time after use and then gently stroked into shape, before being left to dry somewhere where they cannot be knocked out of shape. Failure to do this will mean that a great deal of the spring will be lost from the hair, and it will probably also become split and therefore be quite useless.

A brush which is continually left wet after cleaning will soon start shedding its hairs as they rot off at the base just where they enter the ferrule. So drying a brush is just as important as cleaning it.

A selection of sable and hog oil brushes, although the flat sables serve as very good 'one stroke' poster brushes.

Generally speaking, there is a different range of brushes for watercolours, oils and signwriting. In the case of watercolour brushes it always pays to buy red sable. Although they are the most expensive they will repay the outlay by staying in shape and lasting longer than all others. There are two main shapes favoured by watercolourists: chisel-ended and rounds. The chisel-ended are used mainly for laying on larger areas of colour and washes, while the rounds are used for smaller and more detailed work.

Oil-colour brushes are normally either white hog-hair or sable. The hog-hair is much stiffer than the sable and so will not lend itself to such smooth and subtle work. This is not a criticism of hog-hair brushes, as they are most important to the oil painter.

Good-quality signwriting brushes are also made from red sable, but there are also squirrel and synthetic ones; all have very long hairs, although the actual length does depend on the style, and they are chisel-ended. They come in the usual range of sizes and also in an enormous selection of qualities and styles. And there is a choice of metal-ferruled or quill-mounted hair. All brushes have varnished or painted wooden handles, and generally speaking all are about the same length, with the exception of oil brushes, which often tend to be a little longer in the handle to allow the artist to stand away from the canvas while painting.

If you are using acrylics you can use any type of brush that suits you, but it is more important than ever that you should thoroughly clean them immediately you have finished work.

You might find it a good idea as I do – keep one jar for watercolour brushes and another for oil brushes, or signwriting brushes. If you keep them all together, you would be surprised how frustrating it can be, looking for one particular brush.

Coloured Pencils

Everyone has used coloured pencils at some time or other, but not everyone has persevered with them until they are capable of producing finished artwork. They do have a use in their own right and are especially useful for preparing coloured roughs. They are also used extensively by illustrators for putting the final detail onto painted artwork, mainly watercolour and gouache. However, the purchasing of a set of coloured pencils should be done with a lot of thought and care because this is not necessarily a case where the most expensive is the best. Some makes have much harder leads than others and consequently are that much more difficult to use, especially on hard or smooth surfaces. Sometimes the cheaper pencils with softer leads will produce more 'colour', and this is essential when using them to tighten up a painting. There are a good many makes to choose from, with something like 72 colours in a complete range.

(*above and below*). Coloured pencils are not only fast and therefore ideal for preparing roughs and layouts, but they have a quality all of their own which a lot of artists use to advantage.

Lacones - Corfu - 1977

Pencils

The word 'pencil' comes from the Latin 'penicillum' – a little tail – and even today among professionals a thin brush with long tapering hairs is known as a pencil. However, pencils as they are generally known these days come in two sorts: either the 'lead' is encased in a wooden holder producing the ubiquitous pencil; or it is held in position by some mechanical arrangement such as the standard clutch pencil or the special clutch pencil. The great difference is that the ordinary wooden pencil has to be sharpened periodically and the type of point the artist requires has to be fashioned by a blade. On the other hand, the standard clutch pencil has no wood to shave away to expose the lead, although a special sharpener is used which can put a needle-sharp point on in next to no time. This is ideal for detailed work, and very controllable. The special clutch pencil is not usually sharpened at all because the lead is much thinner (0.3 mm, 0.5 mm or 0.7 mm), and therefore the width of the line can remain consistantly thin without sharpening. All leads for all pencils come in a range of softness/hardness which in effect means a range of blackness.

The alsatian was drawn with a charcoal pencil. It produces a dense black line which reproduces well. The texture of the paper you work on with this medium is very important and is largely responsible for the final result.

Whereas the alsatian is reproduced as 'line' work, the heads are 'half-tone' because of the shades of grey in between black and white. The heads were drawn in pencil over a watercolour wash background. There is also a little stump blending to go along with the wash.

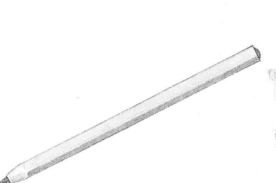

The ball-pen can be used rather like a pencil because the variations in pressure on the pen produce a line of varying density, therefore for reproduction it will have to be half-toned.

The stylo (or technical) pen, which generally uses a black waterproof ink, produces a line of consistent width and density and is much used for method drawings and diagrams. As this type of pen has its own reservoir, some artists use it as a sketching pen. They come in a wide range of widths.

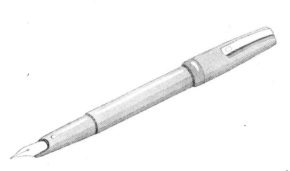

The sketching pen (which has a very expressive nib) and is fillable, is ideal for the traditional pen drawing as it produces lines much like the dip-pen, without the dipping.

2 EQUIPMENT

Drawing Boards

I find generally that there is not a lot mentioned about drawing boards, and yet this is a fundamental piece of equipment, without which it is difficult to make a start on any type of work – almost everything starts at 'drawing board stage'. You will need at least two drawing boards, and probably three or four. First of all a large drawing board is a must; as large as you can get and accommodate. The reason is that from time to time large jobs *do* crop up, and if you haven't got a drawing board large enough you will find it exceedingly difficult to handle. Anyway, you can always do small jobs on a large drawing board, or perhaps two jobs at the same time using the same tee square for instance. A second drawing board can be of more modest proportions, say 30 in (75 cm) square, and then a smaller one still which could be considered portable.

There are various reasons for having more than one drawing board, the most common being that you can have more than one job on hand at the same time and if necessary you can switch from job to job without setting them up each time. A thickish piece of plywood makes a perfectly good board providing it is given a couple of coats of varnish first. This makes it easier to keep clean and also gives the fixing tape a better surface to grip.

Tee-Squares

Naturally a perfectly straight left-hand edge to the drawing board is a pre-requisite for a tee-square. Make sure the arm of the tee-square measures roughly the width of the drawing board. There is not much point in having an arm that is either a lot longer than the width or a lot shorter. It follows that it would be ideal if each drawing board had its own matching tee-square.

Rulers

More than one length of ruler is useful too. An 18 in or 24 in (45 or 60 cm) plastic one with parallel lines marked down the middle is a great boon in helping to get lines straight. A short ruler also is most useful, perhaps a 6 in (15 cm) one as this can be moved about quickly over the work and used at all angles when a complicated mechanical drawing is being worked, for instance. Never use one of your rulers as a cutting edge; for one thing you are sure to cut nicks out of it which will render it practically useless, and for another thing it is not thick enough to be safe – a piece of plastic curtain track is ideal.

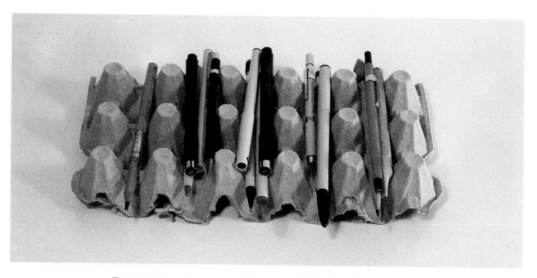

The egg carton shown here works very well. It holds a lot of pencils and pens etc. and you can have whatever size you like within reason. If you are working on a sloping drawing board you can tape the egg stand down on the board and then things don't slip about. In this situation it will also hold pots and tubes and is also good for resting brushes in while they are in use.

If you can make your own light box, think carefully about its size before you start. Remember it has to be convenient to work at and also be big enough for your sort of work. Use a fluorescent tube as illumination as these give a more even distribution of light and remain cooler in use than tungsten.

Light-Box

The light-box seems to be much underrated by books that include it (if only just to mention it). The fact is that light-boxes can be a tremendous asset to any commercial studio. Apart from the most common use, i.e. to examine colour transparencies and colour separations, plus negatives and overlays, other uses range from making final drawings from the original rough sketches once they are correct; making copies by hand from the first layout (posters, handbills, menus etc); to adapting the box as an illuminated paste-up table. To do this you take a sheet of graph paper and tape it round the edge on top of the working surface of the light-box. Then place a piece of clear acrylic sheet over the top of the graph paper. You now have an illuminated grid which can be used for all make-up work without the aid of a tee-square – much quicker and more accurate.

Whatever illumination you decide on, have plenty of it. There is nothing worse than having to move your work around to get it in a good light. Work done in good bright surroundings always finishes up looking better than work done under poor lighting conditions.

Illumination

This is perhaps not so much 'Equipment' as an absolute necessity. It is the first thing to get right when setting up your studio. Without the light being right, it will be next to impossible to produce good work. Obviously if there is a window in a practical position it should be considered as the starting point for setting up the drawing board or desk. This will be a great deal better than any system of artificial illumination you can devise, just because of the quality of the light. That is not to say that you won't need any extra lights because you almost certainly will, but hopefully only as secondary illumination.

The ideal arrangement (if you are right-handed) is to have the source of light coming in over your left shoulder, and slightly in front – at about say 10 o'clock. This makes sure that you don't work in your own shadow and also that you don't get any glare-back from your paper.

The way you light your studio will depend considerably on the sort of work you do, of course, but I would just like to give a word of warning about fluorescent lights. They do give very good illumination overall and they are very economic, but they can present considerable problems if you are working in colour. So do experiment before you commit yourself.

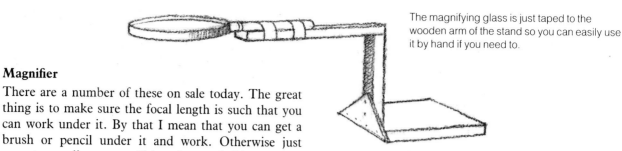

The magnifying glass is just taped to the wooden arm of the stand so you can easily use it by hand if you need to.

Magnifier

There are a number of these on sale today. The great thing is to make sure the focal length is such that you can work under it. By that I mean that you can get a brush or pencil under it and work. Otherwise just mount an ordinary magnifying glass, as I did years ago. I am still using the same one to this day. (See my drawing.)

The mahl sticks speak for themselves I think. Don't make them too long or they become unwieldy and not much use.

Mahl Stick

It is much better in the case of a mahl stick to make your own. This way you will finish up with a superior product, and it will be tailored to your own personal requirements. You must first decide exactly what sort of work you are going to use it for, because this will determine how it is made. If it is a rest for your hand to keep it away from wet paint while you are continuing to work, then a length of dowelling with a wad of cloth tied tightly to the end will do very nicely; the length of the dowelling will depend on the size of the work you are undertaking. If, on the other hand, you need a mahl stick along which you are going to slide your hand or brush in the way a signwriter does, then a wooden metre rule with a piece of sponge taped to the end makes a really excellent one.

All the items on this page are home-made and therefore exactly what I wanted. So often if you have to buy equipment you have to have the nearest you can get. Each one of these pieces is invaluable.

The coathanger compasses work really well because the arms are curved just right for the point and the pencil on the paper.

The bridge can be used for either brush, pen or pencil and can be equally a wrist rest or a straight edge.

Bridge

Bridges are a bit out of fashion now, but are nevertheless very useful for small and precise work. They are used mainly for lining work. The bridge is placed in position over the work, and a long-haired lining brush can be drawn down its edge to produce very straight lines. It is also useful for resting the hand on when working over wet work, as is a mahl stick, but the bridge is used on horizontal surfaces whereas the mahl stick is used mainly on vertical surfaces.

Compasses

Ordinary pairs of compasses are sold everywhere for use by everyone from schoolchildren to architects, but instruments for drawing large circles with pens, markers, chalk or charcoal are a bit more difficult to come by. There are a number of ways, however, of drawing a large circle; a piece of string with a drawing-pin at one end and a pencil at the other – surprisingly accurate, but no good for drawing a circle on a shop window, for instance.

Another method of constructing large circles is to bolt two wooden coat-hangers together, as in my drawing. The pencil (or pen or chalk or whatever) is taped in position at the end of one hanger, and the point (which in this case is a small nail) is taped to the other.

The beam compass can have the point/pencil taped as shown or held by rubber bands in which case the pencil can be moved along without too much trouble. Bulldog clips are also convenient.

As the pantograph needs to be fairly accurately constructed and fairly rigid too, it is usual to buy rather than make. The aluminium ones are very accurate and provide a wide range of scales both enlarging and reducing.

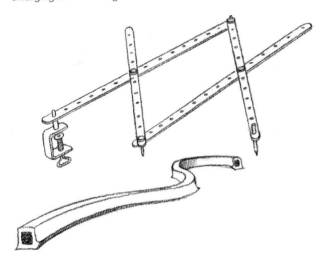

The flexicurve has its limitations in that it won't produce a really tight curve and remain stable. One way round this problem is to tape it into the required position.

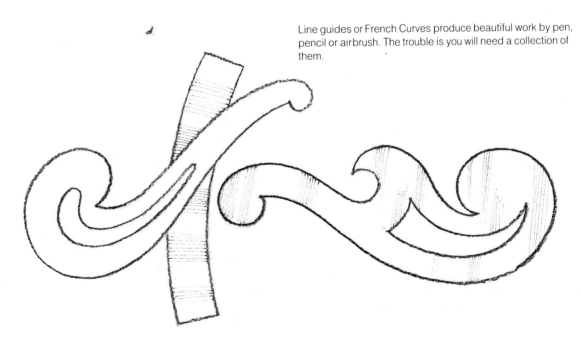

This makes a surprisingly efficient pair of compasses, and when they are required to draw a circle on a sheet of glass or the side of a vehicle all you need is an ordinary eraser, which you hold with your left hand at the centre of the circle; insert the compass point into it and draw the circle in the usual way, still holding the eraser in position.

A beam compass can also be used in the same way. There is hardly any restriction on the length of the beam, and so a circle of almost any radius can be drawn this way.

Pantograph

This is a very cheap and simple instrument for assisting in the making of copies at either the same size or enlarged or reduced in scale. The pantograph is set and anchored at one end. The original copy is placed under the pointer, which is then moved by hand over the contours of the original, whilst the pencil at the end of the other arm draws the new image (at the pre-set size) onto another sheet of paper.

Flexicurve

This is a plastic line-guide that can be adjusted to almost any contour you need. It is ideal for use with pen or pencil.

French Curves

These are rigid plastic shapes for use as pre-set line guides, designed to give as many different types of curves as possible. Usually it is necessary to have a number of these as a set in order to cope with all the variations of curves that may be needed in a precise drawing.

Line guides or French Curves produce beautiful work by pen, pencil or airbrush. The trouble is you will need a collection of them.

Sponges

Sponges come in all shapes and sizes. First of all do make sure you choose a real sponge, and secondly choose the most irregular-shaped one you can find. By doing this you will learn that the sponge can be a very versatile piece of equipment. It can be used for damping water-colour paper prior to stretching, laying on watercolour washes, washing out small areas for correction, stippling, etc.

Erasers

Again there are different erasers for different types of work, so choose the right one for the job. This is more important than perhaps it sounds, because using the wrong eraser can actually ruin the job.

Stumps and Tortillons

These two items are used for the same purpose, i.e. the controlled smudging of pencil or charcoal work. They can either be rubbed over the original work to soften the lines and produce super-smooth shading or they can be dipped into a saucer of pencil or charcoal dust and used directly as a drawing instrument. This gives a very ethereal effect without any lines at all; almost like painting with a pencil. For finer work still, of the same type, cotton buds are found to work quite well, but they don't last very long. Experimentation with different papers is necessary for total success.

These items may seem to be small and trivial but you can never have too many of them. They are all an essential part of the commercial artist's studio. You would be surprised how difficult it is to buy even a good sponge – so when you have a good one, look after it.

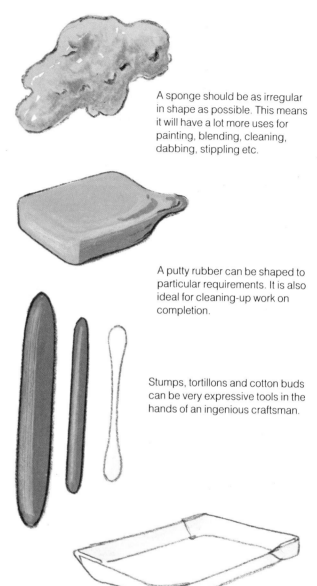

A sponge should be as irregular in shape as possible. This means it will have a lot more uses for painting, blending, cleaning, dabbing, stippling etc.

A putty rubber can be shaped to particular requirements. It is also ideal for cleaning-up work on completion.

Stumps, tortillons and cotton buds can be very expressive tools in the hands of an ingenious craftsman.

A piece of art paper folded as shown makes a fine mixing pallet.

Mixing Palettes and Dishes

Old saucers, pieces of tile, glass and plastic, old jar lids and even odd bits of good card will all do very well as mixing palettes and dishes. Most of the time it pays to use bits of card, because they can be thrown away as soon as they have been used. Indeed, in one studio I worked in many years ago, we always made our own mixing containers from cartridge paper. We cut the paper into about 6 in (15 cm) squares and just bent them up round the edges, as you can see from my sketch. Believe it or not, they held paint for days before they were thrown away.

Sprays

Studio sprays are used mainly for spraying either paint or fixative. The sprays themselves fall into three main types: the mouth spray where your own 'puff' provides the power; the pressurised can or aerosol; and the spray-gun or airbrush. Which you use will depend as ever on the sort of work you do mainly, and partly on your circumstances, because there is an enormous range in price between the mouth-spray and a good airbrush. The mouth-spray is perfectly good for spraying fixative over finished artwork, for instance, and damping water-colour paper, and even spraying colour where the texture is not required to be particularly fine. Aerosols are getting better and are certainly very convenient. They also are used extensively for spraying fixative, as well as varnish and large areas of paint where not too much control or precision is required. Their great use lies in the laying on of areas of flat colour, which they do admirably. It remains for the airbrush to tackle the artistic work, and Chapter 10 deals with this fascinating subject.

Fixative is essential for all pencil or pastel work. It can even be a safeguard over water-soluble inks and paints.

Heavy pencil, charcoal and pastel all need to be 'fixed'

Apart from airbrushing, sprays are probably most commonly used for 'fixing'. Mouth sprays are quite adequate for this and much less expensive. There are also re-fillable aerosols but they do not seem to be totally satisfactory.

Easels and Supports

Easels come either as vertical or horizontal (or adjustable to both) and are made of wood or aluminium in most cases. When buying an easel, don't just choose from a catalogue where they all look good; go along and inspect them closely, because so many are designed for lightness and compactness that sometimes something of the stability and rigidity is lost as a result. The essential requirement of an easel is stability.

Another advantage of the neck strap support for the drawing board is that it can be used to carry the board, satchel fashion, with the strap over the shoulder.

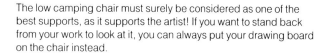

The low camping chair must surely be considered as one of the best supports, as it supports the artist! If you want to stand back from your work to look at it, you can always put your drawing board on the chair instead.

There are other less conventional methods of supporting your work which you may like to consider. One way is to fix a neck-strap to your drawing board – this is quite handy for sketching and making studies, but not a lot of good for painting. Another idea for a lightweight easel is to make use of a camera tripod. Get a suitably-sized piece of plywood and screw to the back in the middle a threaded camera mount. This will enable the board to be screwed onto the tripod in place of the camera and will provide a fully adjustable easel for sketching and a horizontal support for watercolour painting.

Another way to approach outdoor painting is to get hold of a really low garden or camping chair. This should be just a few inches off the ground, so that when you sit in it your knees are fairly drawn up and make a perfect support for your drawing board. This arrangement also means that the ground is within comfortable reaching distance and you can therefore use it as your worktop with all your paints and palettes etc set out around you.

Cord and Drawing Pins

These items might sound to be rather trivial and not worth mentioning here but nothing could be further from the truth. Most artists and designers at some time or other will have been faced with the task of drawing out a large circle or oval; large in this case being anything from 3 feet (1 metre) in diameter or larger.

The method of drawing a circle with a piece of cord attached to a drawing pin at one end (the centre) and held taut with a pencil at the other needs no more explanation, except to say that the method works surprisingly well providing the cord is of good quality and does not stretch.

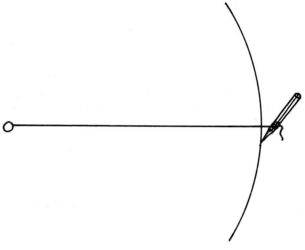

This simple string and pencil method of drawing a circle is quite accurate and really has no size limit.

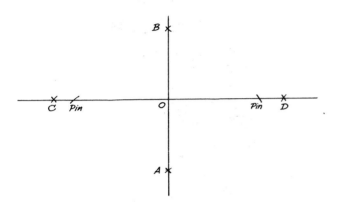

Make sure the pins are firmly fixed in their positions before you start fitting the cord. The amount of strain on them is quite substantial; the tighter you can draw against the cord, the more accurate the oval will be.

Keep the marking tool (pencil, pen) in an upright position all the time or else it won't join up nicely. You need not actually tie the ends of the cord together to form a loop, holding them will serve just as well, especially as it is quite difficult to tie the knot so the loop is exactly the right size.

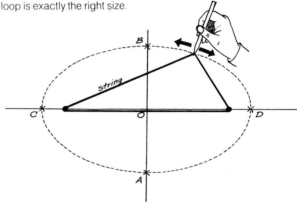

A rubber held in position to take the point of the compasses is a convenient way of drawing a circle on a hard surface such as glass or vehicle side.

As for ovals, the system continues to work very well and produces a delightful ellipse regardless of size, the only snag being the fixing of the pins when working on a hard surface such as glass or metal. The solution to this dilemma is either to mark out the oval on paper first (using the same method of construction) and then trace through onto the working surface, or to push the pins into small blocks of wood which are held in the right position on the working surface with double-sided tape. The decision inevitably has to be decided at the time since many other factors will provide contributing influences.

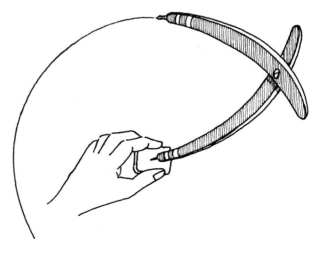

Drying and Finishing

In the winter, especially, the question of how to dry off the finished work is often the biggest question of the day. Generally speaking, an ordinary fan heater is all that is needed, and as they are so compact they can easily be directed to where the warm air is needed most. This is not always suitable, however, for example when there are a considerable number of items to dry off at the same time, and so it is generally more convenient to hang, stack or lay them out of the way somewhere to dry off in their own time. There are a number of ways to do this and you will have to decide which is best for you.

A simple clothes line with either clothes pegs or paper clips to hold the posters, cards, tickets, photos, banners etc is very useful, especially as they can be bought in the form of 'pull-out' lines with five or six individual nylon lines ready for use all at the same time.

The 'washing line' is useful for one or two very good reasons. It costs practically nothing to buy – just a length of nylon line and some small pegs, preferably not the wooden sort because they sometimes stain the work. Otherwise use paper clips. Another advantage is that it can be put in a drawer when it's not in use and also it will accommodate almost any size of work.

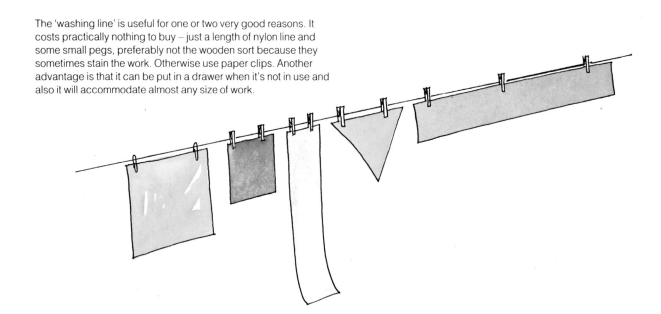

Paper clips are useful for small and light things.

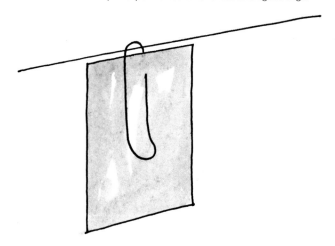

A marbles rack is very efficient and effective if you have a lot of poster work to do. By this method a lot of posters can be safely hung in a small area; in fact they can be hung so close that there is a danger that passers-by might cause enough draught to set them swaying slightly, and if they touch while they are still wet they might produce some 'set-off'. Nevertheless this is a very good way to hang a lot of posters.

The marbles rack does take a little while to make and does have to be fairly accurate as far as the sawing is concerned otherwise it will not work. However if you are fairly handy with wood and tools, it presents no problem at all and is a very good investment.

Side view

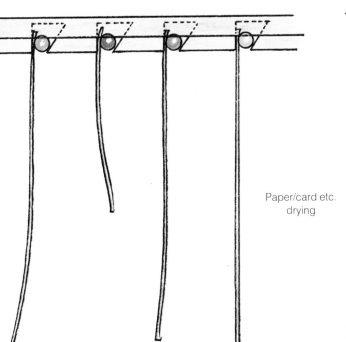

Front view

Paper/card etc. drying

Nailed batten rack

Stiff card and/or boards are conveniently racked by standing them in nailed battens. The great thing about this method is that the battens can be moved closer in or farther out depending on the size of the boards being dried. When they are not wanted they can be picked up and stood in the corner.

A more universal type of drying rack is the one which uses wire trays. These are arranged to slide in and out of a framework which is usually on castors to give it mobility. This sort of rack is so useful in as much as it can accommodate large and/or small jobs without any adjustment or rearrangement, and can easily be made by the handyman with very little in the way of costs for

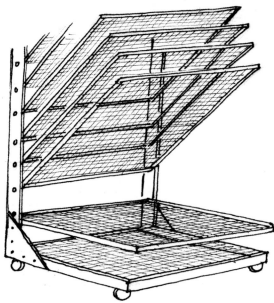

These wire trays are most useful and can be stacked upright when not in use. They are also on castors so they can be brought up close to the printing or writing position.

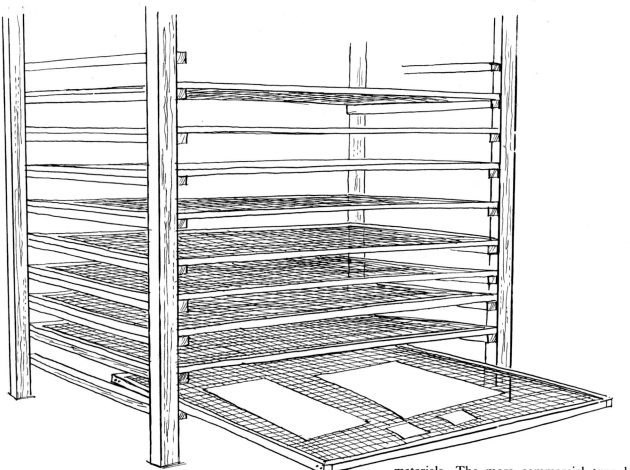

This rack of wire trays is well within the capabilities of the handyman – the drawing says it all.

materials. The more commercial type has its trays hinged and spring-loaded onto the frame at the back, enabling the user to start from the bottom upwards. This means you start with all the trays tipped up, pulling them down as you need them, and so always having a flat tray ready to receive the work. These racks too are mounted on castors, adding to their versatility.

Trimming

Frequently the last operation in the preparation of work is to trim it round. For reasons of handling or colour bleeding, it is more convenient to leave a margin of waste material all round which must be trimmed off at the end. If there are more than a few items that require this sort of attention, a guillotine is a great help, not only because of the saving of time but also because it allows a strip of card to be fixed (by means of double-sided tape) in such a position as to serve as a 'stop' when putting the work into the guillotine. This dispenses with the need to measure each one as you go and yet ensures that each finished article is exactly the same size as the next.

A good hand guillotine will cut a wide selection of materials such as: cartridge-paper, tracing paper, card, mounting board, vinyl, leather, cloth, canvas etc.

A hand operated guillotine.

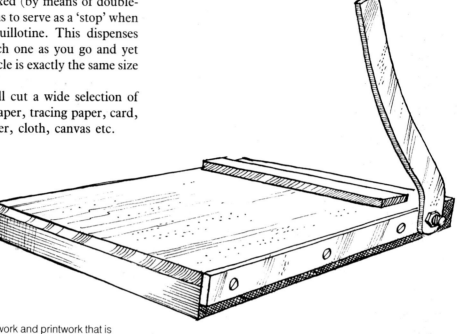

Try to put 'trim marks' on all your artwork and printwork that is going to have to be trimmed. This almost certainly obviates any measuring mistakes by the guillotine operator and if the marks are put on early in the job they will be useful from time to time for others handling the work.

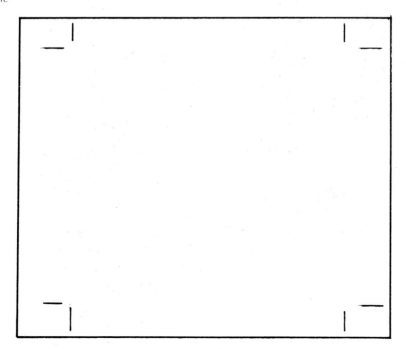

3 WHERE IDEAS COME FROM

I shall keep on emphasising throughout this book the importance of coming up with good original ideas. Customers seldom have good ideas of their own and consequently they rely heavily on the ability of the artist to supply them. If, then, you can evolve some sort of system whereby your mind knows where to start looking when it is given certain requirements by the customer, and at the same time get it down on paper in an attractive way, then you are starting on the road to commercial art.

It is necessary somehow to achieve this continuous flow of ideas straight away. The method we shall adopt will be very similar to that employed in the next chapter on 'References', except that the headings will of course be different. So to begin. Gather up all the magazines, newspapers, brochures, leaflets, business letters, trade journals etc that you can find (it really doesn't matter how outdated they are) and sit down with a pair of scissors and work methodically through them. To start with you should cut out anything that catches your eye, for whatever reason. You are looking for interesting or unusual lettering, smart or clever layout, and original and exciting ideas. Cut out anything that is likely to stimulate you into producing something of your own. Go on cutting out until you have much too much, and don't just rely on publications from your own country because foreign advertisements can be very useful in that they have a slightly different look about them, which will help your interpretation look that much more original.

When you have cut yourself out a great stack of 'scraps', sort them into some sort of classification, i.e. those that you think will lend themselves to being redesigned into letterheads, book jackets, company livery, general advertising, point-of-sale displays etc. But remember – these are *not* for copying; they are for the idea only, and as such they will save you hours and hours of unproductive time.

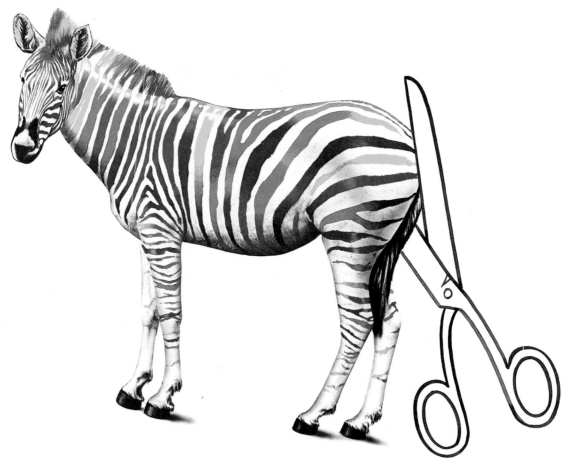

Some of the usual run of letterheads. Any of the ideas could easily be used in another way for something else.

For instance, let's start with what is probably the most often asked-for bit of artwork – namely the letterhead. Businesses rely very heavily on their image (which is largely what this book is all about) and nothing conveys an image better than a letterhead. Look through your cuttings with your eyes while your mind is concentrating on the letterhead you are eventually going to design. Remember, you are not looking for something to copy – only an idea that will set you off on the road to an original design. Page 40 will show you what I mean.

Here is a simple and bold design that looks equally well as a letterhead, business card, vehicle livery and facia.

When you think you have discovered a good idea you should try to get it down on paper, in rough form only at first. Then try working on it from another angle; or better still, try another idea and get that down on paper too, also in rough form. The reason for preparing two or three different roughs is so that your client can choose for himself (which makes him think that he has had a hand in the whole thing) which one he prefers, and also it helps to ensure that you have given the whole idea a fair amount of your imagination – for which you can charge a better fee. I always do two or more roughs unless I think I have got a winner in the first one, and then I don't bother with any more in case the client chooses one of the others! Incidentally, it is a well-known fact that too big a choice will confuse and therefore perhaps blight the whole commission.

Once you have got the letterhead right there is normally a natural progression of work throughout the customer's business that will automatically call for your services, i.e. he will want the same design transferred to the rest of his stationery (business cards, invoices, compliments slips, etc), and then on to his vehicles, shop fronts and general advertising. This shows why it is so vitally important to get the letterhead right, and to establish a good relationship with the customer at an early stage.

It may be just a simple logo you design, but if it is good it will probably be used throughout the customer's business.

It might be as well to bear in mind that a design/idea that was not particularly successful with one customer does not necessarily mean that it will not be successful with the next. My example on this page shows this quite clearly.

IDEAS will come from practically anywhere and everywhere. One thing will lead to another to another in a kind of chain. One idea that starts out being one thing finishes up as something quite different.

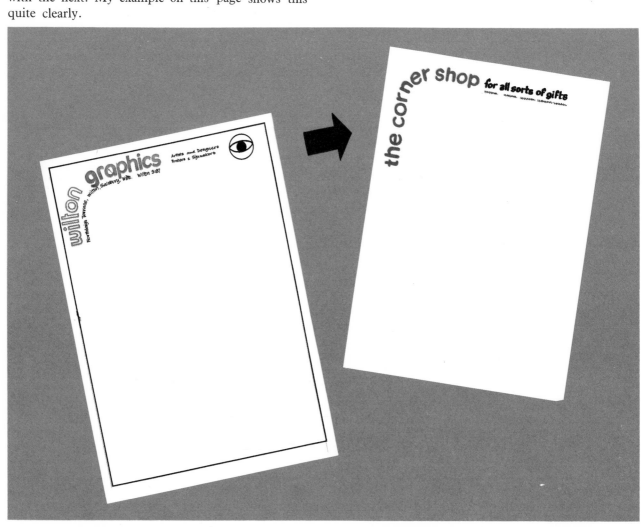

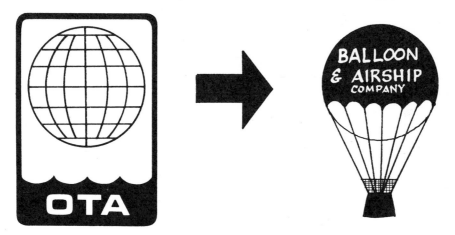

Another example of how 'one thing leads to another'.

Another source of ideas comes from the small ads found in the back of most large magazines and papers. You will soon get to know which publications carry the most useful advertisements, and these will not only give you ideas but also a valuable selection of layouts and lettering. Tear a few pages out and browse through them from time to time. Surround yourself with bits of paper of lettering, layout, colourings and so on and you will be surprised to find how quickly your mind starts to help you sort out what might be useful and what won't!

Some pages of small ads are more lucrative than others. You will soon get to know where the best ones occur. It is often worth buying a particular magazine or paper just for the adverts...there is no cheaper way of buying ideas anywhere.

Yet another source of ideas is the unpredictable one; the one that comes at the most unlikely time, for instance when watching TV, reading a book, out walking or listening to somebody talking (because, remember, ideas are not necessarily visual or graphic, but can be descriptive as well).

This is a good example of an idea that worked well. The photograph is of my own bathroom wallpaper, and the logo resulting from it was very successful.

The natural development from bathroom wallpaper to tea rooms letterhead.

In order to make the most of your potential as a commercial artist with original ideas, you must become adept at translating ideas from one medium to another. For instance, you might be attracted to a particularly well-coloured wallpaper pattern in a friend's house, and notice how one individual motif in that pattern would make a very good symbol or logo for your customer's flower shop. Or again you might be listening to a conversation in a restaurant where someone is describing the view from their balcony when they were on holiday last. As a result of this you may conjure up a mental picture of exactly the sort of scene you need to illustrate a book on smuggling.

An illustration from a book on smuggling.

Ideas can come from Yellow Pages or posters – although they may not be good enough for references they are full of good ideas.

5763-A

5975-A

4893-A

GET A GOOD GRIP THAT WON'T SLIP

GET TO THE MIDDLE OF THINGS THE ENDS ARE PINCHPOINTS

WATCH OUT FOR PINCH POINTS

these hazards could lurk anywhere...

keep ha CLE

4558-

BROKEN GLASS DON'T PICK IT UP!

KEYSTONE OF A GOOD STACK

ISP/L12-1

30"×20"

STACK PALLETS SAFELY

ISP/L24-1

30"×20"

BONDED

ISP/L25-1

FOR SAFETY

30"×20"

Tidiness

Dispose of glass... Carefully

TIDY UP

ISP/B62-1

30"×20"

Clearway

IN WORKSHOPS CLEARWAYS ARE SAFEWAYS

ISP/H49-1

Poster catalogues are rich in ideas for colours and words as well as artwork.

Once you have developed the 'Seeing Eye' ideas will come from everywhere . . .

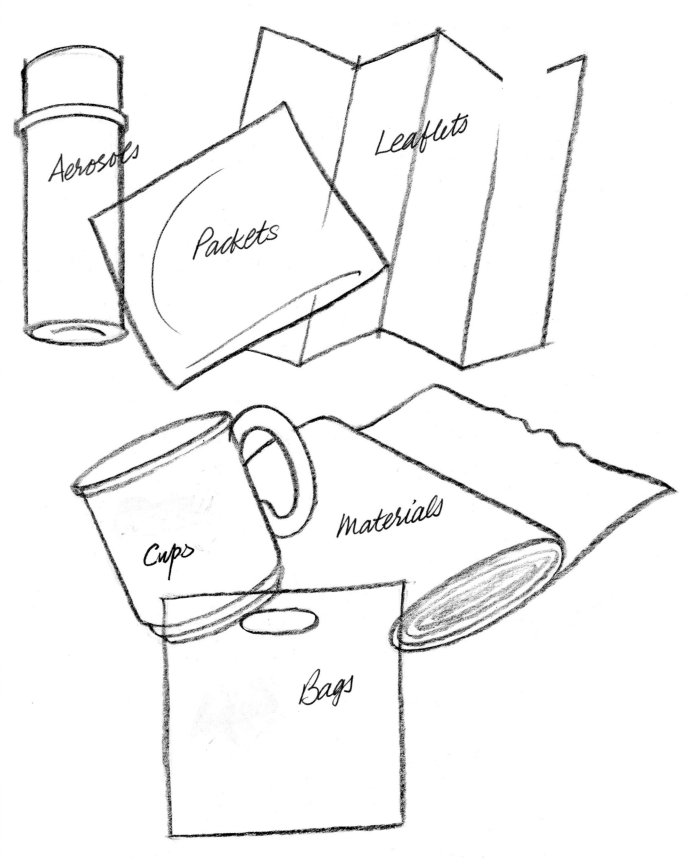

Aerosols

Leaflets

Packets

Cups

Materials

Bags

. . . and so on until you can't get away from them!

THE HALCYON TIME FOR EVER
The beautifully-named kingfisher looks over his
territory in the pride of his plumage and in
somewhere, in a hole in the ri...

Barn Owl

WORLD

...ess beauty in the classical style

...ILLUSTRATED staff photographers. Karsh is
...character studies of famous men, but some
...I put to as successful with women. They're
...own here are masterpieces—beautifully posed
...Burn he shows against every... in Extend the
...reception of glamour—windswept and vital

Here I am
and I'm a blonde
Blonde as sunshine
and I just want to
burst out laughing. And,
all because I used Hiltone,
everything's happening
and I feel like
taking off.

It's a blonde's life!
Thanks, Hiltone!

hiltone

SUNDAY

MONDAY

4 REFERENCES

'An artist is only as good as his references' is so often heard and so true. The great thing to remember about keeping references is only to keep the good ones. It is so easy to hoard vast quantities of cats, dogs, faces and figures, without giving much thought to the merit of the picture. Ordinary 'run-of-the-mill' references are not good enough because they are available to everybody – they make you no better than the next commercial artist … and you must aim to be better at all costs. A really good reference, therefore, gives you a head start in producing a first-class bit of artwork. A poor reference, on the other hand, leaves a lot to be done by the artist by way of imagination or guesswork, neither of which can be relied on for accuracy.

As these references are going to be so important in our lives, we must choose a suitable method of keeping them. I start by suggesting a collection of flat boxes, say five or six, each with a label on the outside describing the type of pictures inside. This is the way I have kept my references for the last 30 years and there are still some cuttings among them now that were in my original collection. Needless to say, they have been used over and over again in various ways during all those years. The attraction of this system is that it is the easiest! There is no mounting or trimming or any other form of preparation – just snip them out and put them in the box.

A much more attractive way of keeping your cuttings is in a scrap book. This is undoubtedly a much tidier method and much easier to use when you are looking for something. Scrap books are even just nice to look through occasionally, but they *are* a little bit more trouble to keep going. Also it must be said in their favour that they are a lot nicer to have around the studio – they look a lot more professional. But, for all that, they are not so easy to work from as a single cutting taken from the box.

Children's Encyclopedias

These are a wonderful source of inspiration altogether. Not only are they good visual references, but they are descriptive as well. This means that there is often a description of where the subject is usually found, or where it lives, or how it compares in size, for instance, and this must serve as a great help to the artist if he wants to include a bit of background to his subject, or place it in its proper environment. Large parts of these children's encyclopedias don't date very quickly, and they can be obtained from most second-hand book-shops quite cheaply.

Whichever method you use – fill them up. The system doesn't become really useful until it has a lot in it. A casual look through sometimes reminds you of things you had completely forgotten about and gives you a whole new train of thought.

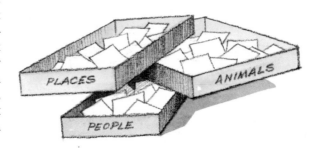

This illustrates, the sort of encylopedias that are worth having. Plenty of good illustrations and descriptive text.

Postcards

These are useful mainly as references of places, although cards that are sold in museums, art galleries and exhibitions are most valuable and often can't be purchased elsewhere.

Travel Brochures

These are a marvellous place to start looking for palm trees, mountain scenery, figures, exotic views and dramatic skies. Some time ago I needed a picture of a Mississippi paddle steamer; I went straight to the nearest travel agent and got exactly what I needed – so easy.

There is so much printed material about these days that you will have no trouble collecting interesting items and you will soon start being selective.

Mail-Order Catalogues

For any of the 'everyday' household items, these books have got it all! From kettles and coffee mugs to radios, cameras and watches, it's all there in the clearest possible form. Also, and this is of the utmost importance, it's all bang up to date.

Another reminder that mail order catalogues give you some very good posed figures, male, female and children. Not much in the way of action but most useful for casual poses.

Sketch Books

This is probably the oldest method of keeping references. The advantage of keeping a sketch book for this purpose is that it is fun to do and absolutely unique. Added to which, these days, artists' sketch books are much sought after and therefore command quite a high price, so you will be investing your time and talents in two ways at the same time.

Do use your sketchbook as much as you can. Preferably a small one because a large one becomes a hindrance and so tends to get left behind. If you can get into the habit of always taking a little sketchbook wherever you go, it will soon get filled up with useful work and you will improve your skills at the same time.

Camera and Polaroid Camera

This is probably the newest method of preparing references, and there is very little that needs to be said. A polaroid-type camera can save you an enormous amount of time in making a record of something. In fact, when I once had to repaint a coat of arms, high up above a rather grand doorway, I started by taking my instant camera up and taking a careful central shot of it. I then just took one measurement (across the middle) and the rest of it I was able to scale up from that one measurement in my studio.

Any assistance that you can contrive is the name of the game. Remember, others who were better than you have done it; some of them could not have managed without it.

Written Notes

Written notes on colour, sizes, materials and textures are sometimes more helpful and even more accurate than an illustrative attempt, especially so when you are on location, because all you need for written notes is a pencil; whereas if you were to make a graphic reference you would need certain equipment and paraphernalia, which in some situations may prove difficult to manage. Written notes are particularly useful when you are trying to capture a mood or atmosphere which may be a transient thing, leaving no time for setting up equipment.

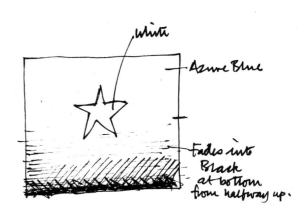

Picture Libraries

This is the source from which most illustrators, authors and publishers get their pictures. There are a number of these libraries to choose from, some specialising in a particular subject or subjects, so you need to approach the right one. Reference to the *Writers' and Artists' Yearbook*, published by A. and C. Black, will prove helpful, and this book is available from your local library.

This book is well worth having by you as it is useful in so many ways. It includes art agents and studios, codes of conduct, copyright, societies and clubs.

Public Library

This is always the first place to try for a reference, and if you are lucky enough to live near a large library you are almost certain to find something to help you in your particular quest. As well as the lending library there is also the reference library where you can browse through the books on your subject to your heart's content. It is helpful to remember that you can usually have any relevant page in a book photocopied on the spot.

Technical leaflets can be a help sometimes. As these are usually free it is well worth keeping your eyes open for them.

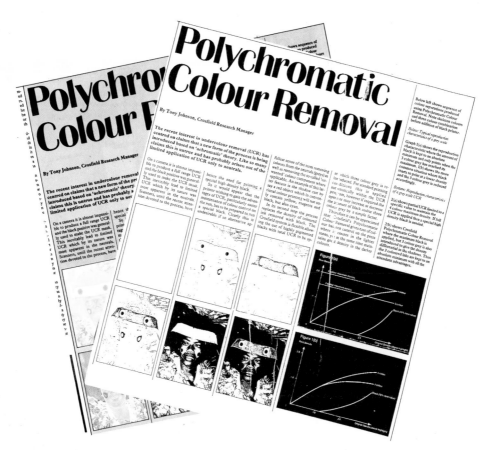

Manufacturer's Leaflets

For specialist work this is a good source, and you can be sure it will be accurate, up-to-date and free. Most manufacturers (or their agents) are only too pleased to give away literature advertising their products, and they are normally most helpful in every way.

For accuracy and detail manufacturers' leaflets are obviously the perfect source. Bear in mind that design and technology change so quickly that it would be wise to use up-to-date literature every time.

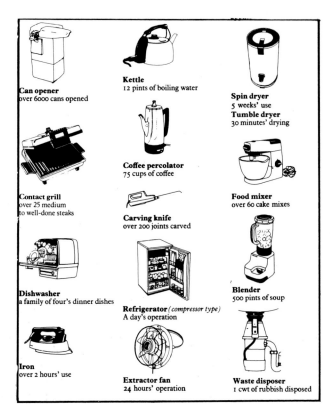

Can opener
over 6000 cans opened

Contact grill
over 25 medium
to well-done steaks

Dishwasher
a family of four's dinner dishes

Iron
over 2 hours' use

Kettle
12 pints of boiling water

Coffee percolator
75 cups of coffee

Carving knife
over 200 joints carved

Refrigerator *(compressor type)*
A day's operation

Extractor fan
24 hours' operation

Spin dryer
5 weeks' use

Tumble dryer
30 minutes' drying

Food mixer
over 60 cake mixes

Blender
500 pints of soup

Waste disposer
1 cwt of rubbish disposed

Sports Sections of Newspapers

These are obviously very good for figures in action. It is quite amazing how often you can use good action figures to liven up what might otherwise be a very dull poster or advertisement. These sorts of figures lend themselves to a variety of treatments, from seemingly hastily-made pen or pencil sketches full of 'speed', to more solid filled-in colour work. Whichever it is, without a good reference to start with it is next to impossible to produce a convincing piece of artwork.

As you may guess, the drawing of the batsman took only about 5 minutes to do from the photograph, but it served the purpose perfectly and was 'professionally acceptable'.

Advertisements

Everybody looks at advertisements (which is what they are supposed to do) because of the eye-catching artwork. So this would seem to be another area from which to cull our references. And so it is, with certain reservations, because although the artwork is usually of a very high standard professionally it is often deliberately exaggerated in some way, and we need to beware of that. Bearing that in mind, advertisements become a veritable cornucopia for us, not only for the items they depict but also for the style they use.

Remember 'style', because I shall come back to that in a later chapter – it is most important. The great value of advertisements to the commercial artist is that an advert for car tyres by a manufacturer will serve very well as a general reference for just a car tyre. Likewise a beer advert will provide a good reference for a can (or bottle); it doesn't really matter what the label says it is. Supermarket ads in the newspapers too are very handy, because they also show how to draw packets, bottles, cans, boxes, meats, cheeses and the like.

Good, clean line ads are a godsend. You can copy them easily or even trace them. If necessary they can be used as the basis for something similar, with the alterations drawn in. This saves a lot of work in setting out the whole drawing from scratch.

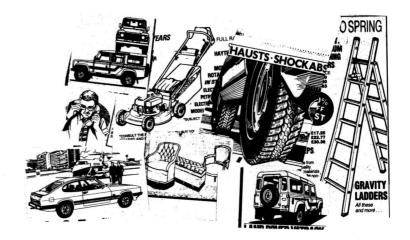

Lettering

Adverts are, of course, as much a source of inspiration for lettering as for illustration. It is very important that exactly the right sort of lettering is chosen to suit the product and the illustration. It can even improve the overall look of the artwork if you get it absolutely right. You will find that all lettering really falls into two categories: recognised typestyles and handwritten. There is more about this in Chapter 11.

Layout

In Chapter 3, I suggested that pages of small ads should be kept as inspiration for these ideas. In the same way now, I would recommend that we keep adverts for closer attention. That is so that we can study things like colour combination, proportions and style. An advertisement which pleases you must do so for some reason; so analyse it to find out why, and then try to repeat the ingredients in your own version.

Advertisements can be kept just for the idea.

5 WHAT ARE ROUGHS?

Roughs or 'visuals' are usually the first sighting the customer has of the artist's attempt to translate onto paper what until now has probably just been an idea in the back of his head. Generally speaking, this is the hard bit – getting off on the right track. In my school days there used to be a saying 'All's well that ends well', but in practice I find it is more true to say 'All's well that starts well', and nowhere does that apply more aptly than in the studio.

If you can produce this first graphic interpretation of the client's wishes satisfactorily or, even better still, produce something that is an improvement on his idea,

then you have jumped one of the biggest hurdles, in that he will have a positive attitude to your work, and life will be a lot easier for you from that moment onwards. If, on the other hand, you find it difficult or you take a long time to get your rough idea right for him, then he may begin to show a slightly negative approach to your work, and this may be the start of a long uphill struggle with your customer. Eventually, what is more important of course is that at the end of the job it will be much more difficult to present him with his account if you know he is not entirely happy with the way you have handled his work.

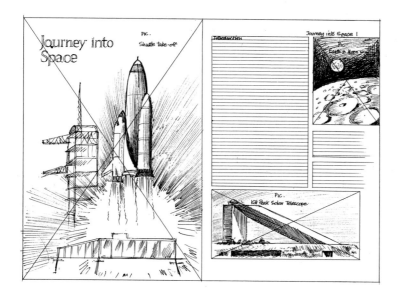

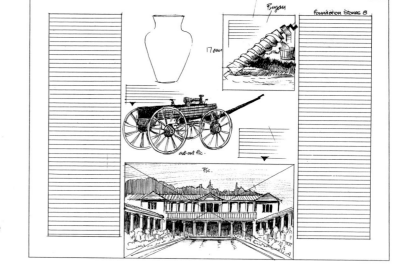

Roughs are sometimes in colour and sometimes in black and white. The roughs shown here are pretty rough although they are still accurate enough to work from, i.e. the pictures are the right size and the text is the right width. It means that artwork can be commissioned and text can be set from it.

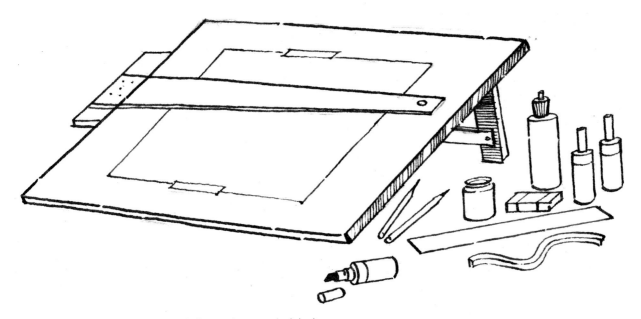

It is surprising what few tools are needed to produce good original designs and roughs. The essential requirement is to be practical.

The golden rule, then, is: get it right from the beginning.

In some cases the client is able to jot down on paper some idea of what it is he wants, which is obviously very helpful, as in the case shown here where the author of this children's encyclopedia sketched out his own roughs for me to work from.

Again, this author is no artist but nevertheless his rough was perfectly sufficient to allow the artist to start work. His drawings were in the right place and the right size and more to the point, it told the artist quite clearly what he wanted.

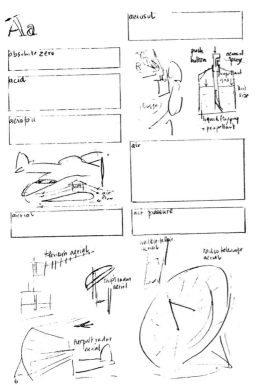

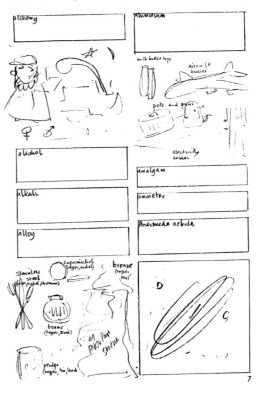

Roughs, by the way, should not be too 'rough'. Indeed they should be quite accurate as far as measurement and colour are concerned, otherwise there is not a lot of point in doing them at all. Roughs are only rough in as much as the artwork has not at this stage had the time spent on it to bring it up to the high standard that you personally can achieve.

One word of warning here: your first design may be anything from a shop facia or bus side to a business card or letterhead.

These roughs in colour are about average for neatness and therefore the time spent on them was also about average.

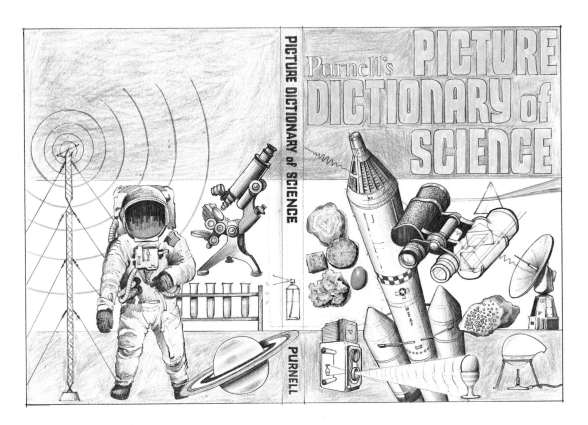

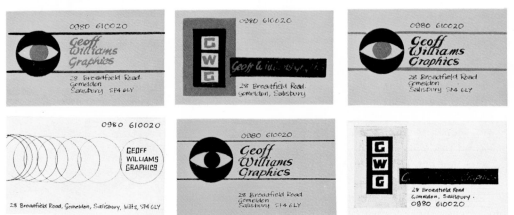

I do not usually produce this many choices for a customer to choose from but in this particular case I was specifically asked to do so.

60

As in all spheres there are fashions that come and go, and in this particular field of roughs it is very fashionable at the moment to do them with marker pens. This is a very quick way of producing coloured layouts, and if you can become slick in the use of them they do produce very stylish artwork. So much so in fact that you have to be very careful when you are doing the finished work that you don't lose the freshness and spontaneity that the original sketch had. However, if you find you don't get on all that well with markers or fibre-tip pens, then use some other medium that suits you better. Use whatever you feel you can handle best to portray your ideas, whether it be coloured pencils, watercolour, inks or gouache.

Once you are quite sure you know what the customer wants, arrange a working schedule – and stick to it! Then get to work.

Your rough layout may not be all handwork; it may well be a pot-pourri of pictures, artwork, lettering and text – in fact it usually is. The pictures may be in the form of photographs which you will fix in position with some sort of low-tack adhesive; the artwork will be sketched in in a representational way; the lettering (headings, slogans, punchlines etc) may be indicated by hand or else by one of the instant lettering systems such as Letraset. The text is normally shown as a column of horizontally straight lines, or perhaps a random column of text cut from another publication just to show where the area of text will be (it doesn't matter what the words say at this stage). Actually the same approach can be adopted with the pictures (if the photograph is not yet available); just use part of any picture from a newspaper or magazine to give the impression of your photograph. It really is quite fun choosing a random photograph for a rough, and it is surprising how close you can get to the finished picture.

Often, having reached this first stage in your design, you will find that alternatives come into your head and you will want to show these as well. The usual method is to use 'overlays'. The alternative is made on a separate piece of paper which is placed in position over the original, and taped down on one side so that it is hinged and can be flipped over the original as often as required for the client to make up his mind.

When you have finished your rough, mount it on card (if you have done it on paper); this makes it convenient to handle and keeps it stiff so that the customer can stand it up and view it from a distance. It also enables you to fix a protective overlay over the whole job, and you can also stick your logo or symbol with your telephone number in the corner.

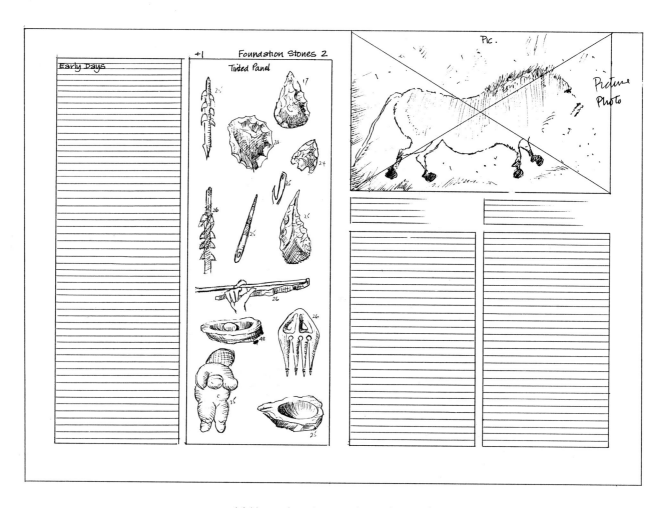

A fairly usual way to present a rough spread.

Another rough spread without marking in the text lines, only indicating with a box where they should be.

Hinged flaps on the artwork serve as a good way to show alternatives. Try to make them neat so they don't distract the eye too much when looking at the overall design.

You will have gathered that there are really two types of rough. There is the visual rough, mainly for the customer's sake so that he can see more or less what he is going to get and there is the working rough, which as the name suggests is for the benefit of those involved in producing the work.

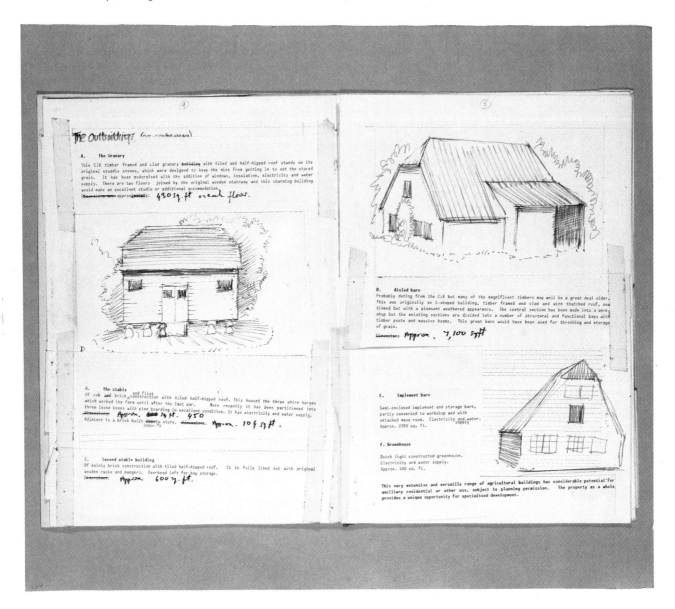

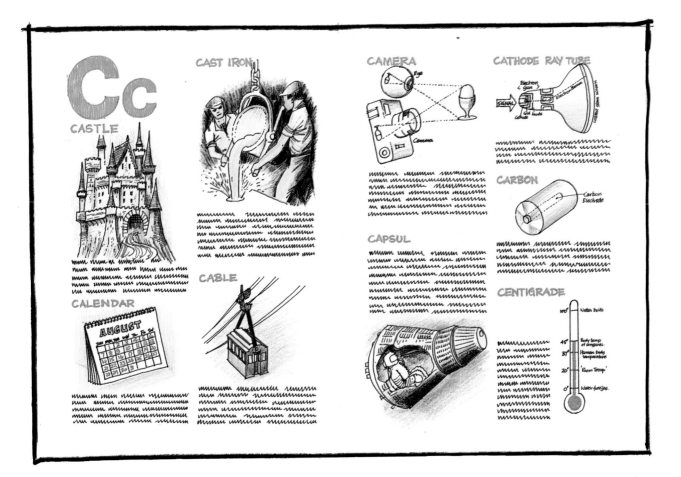

An actual mock-up book is usually the next stage and allows room for a lot more detail to be entered, such as the actual size of photographs and drawings. It also begins to present a visual image of what it is going to look like as opposed to just considering the mechanics.

The flow chart for this book started like this. There were several updatings as time went on, but this was the original plan.

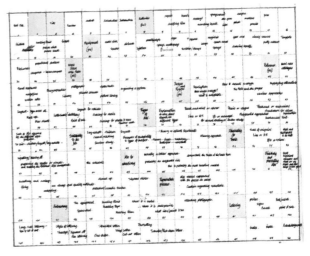

Layouts and roughs for most things are straight-forward enough and can all be produced in this way, but magazines, books, brochures and the like (things with a number of pages) have to be handled a bit differently. For instance, in the case of a book where there are normally a good many pages, the very first step on the part of the designer/artist is to prepare a 'flow chart'. This is a fairly large sheet of paper which is divided into boxes to represent all the pages. It makes it easier to understand if you rule alternate vertical lines a bit heavier to represent the spreads (left-hand and right-hand page when the book is open) but remember when you do this that odd page numbers are always on the right-hand side and even numbers on the left.

Having constructed the flow chart you can now plan the book by jotting in on each page what you intend should go there. The advantage of starting this way is that everybody concerned can see at a glance how the book is planned, and it makes it so easy to re-arrange the layout without juggling with a lot of papers. When the general plan is agreed it is customary then to produce a few sample spreads. These spreads will show in more detail how the pages themselves are going to look. They will show the text and picture areas fairly accurately because the 'setting' (typesetting) and artwork can all be commissioned in accordance with these page layouts.

This is a rough paste-up using a photograph, a piece cut from another publication and rough pencilling by hand.

A spread of the finished book showing revisions incorporated.

Designing for signs and displays requires a certain amount of specialist knowledge, inasmuch as it would be foolish to produce a visually good layout if it was going to be either almost impossible to produce in practice or too expensive anyway. Therefore start by considering the materials that would be suitable and available for the sign and its location. Having settled on this, then go ahead with the design which will generally be a scaled-down drawing of the real thing.

I would strongly advise that you make your layout in the form of a perspective drawing showing the sign in its immediate surroundings. This is a great help to most customers because they generally are not able to visualise the finished product, and they therefore appreciate this bit of extra help. It also gives you an excuse to exercise your artistic talents! A good alternative to this is to take a photograph of the site where the sign is to be erected, whether it is free-standing or otherwise, and paint the sign in with gouache. This is a very effective and quick way of showing precisely how it will look. You can use this system for all sorts of designing – lorry and bus sides, point-of-sale displays in stores, and even artists' impressions of building developments; a good large photographic print of the site before the development, with your painting of the new buildings painted directly onto the photograph, produces a very convincing visual. Incidentally, when working on photographs, whether just retouching or actually doing artwork, do make sure the surface is absolutely grease-free. One fingerprint can spoil all the work you have done. So give the print a good hard rub over with a new tissue, which should do the trick, but if you still find it difficult to get the paint to take, add one drop of washing-up liquid to your colour and your problem will be solved.

A photograph with the prospective sign gouached in to show positioning and scale.

Designs and layouts for posters need to have a moment's consideration before you start. If the posters are ultimately to be printed, then of course you will consider the various typefaces and indicate them on your layout, but if they are to be handwritten or screenprinted you will not necessarily have to consider this point – much better to design for a 'freer' and more characterful arrangement of lettering. Remember that if the posters are going to be handwritten (and it's much more economic if there are only going to be a few, or if they are very large, and also if there are going to be a lot of colours) you want to use lettering that is easy and fast to do. Style is the keyword for posters. Bear in mind also the standard paper sizes – this is very important as you can lose a lot of profit in offcuts of paper, both in the time spent cutting and in the actual wastage of the paper itself.

You will most likely have to do a considerable amount of practising with various brushes and pens, inks and paints before you arrive at a good quick professional style. One of the other important ingredients is good colour combinations. Bad colourings can make even good lettering look unattractive.

These are two roughs for safety campaign posters. You may have to produce a number of such roughs before your client approves one, but it really is the only way.

Brochures and guides usually require a little more thought and in consequence are very satisfying to the artist, now especially so as more and more colour is being used in advertising (which is what this really is) which in turn is giving the designer more and more scope for his talents. This is another worthwhile area in which to work, because naturally brochures and guides are always being updated, which is good news for all concerned. Brochures in particular are very colourful and tend to use colour pictures fairly extensively. As far as the designer is concerned, these start life as transparencies, and so if you have been commissioned by your client to produce a brochure including the pictures you will eventually have to provide the printer with the necessary transparencies – either taken by you or for you.

If you are working in a limited number of colours, it is all the more important to choose those that are complementary and also in keeping with the subject of your work.

Even the small jobs need to be original, interesting and effective.
It is often very difficult to come up with something new every time,
but at least it can be made more effective by the use of the right
colours, type styles, paper and general design.

Designing for cards is fairly straightforward as far as the business, seasonal and greetings range goes. Don't forget to make them fit the standard envelope sizes and take into account the way they will fold. As always when you are designing for a production run the number of colours you use is crucial to the economics. Naturally the cheapest form of reproduction is 'line work', i.e. a design produced in hard black lines as with a pen, whether it be stylo, dip or roller. Even this can be made to look very attractive by printing on coloured or textured paper. (The sequence of little drawings on page 00 was done with a stylo pen on coloured paper.)

These cards were all black and white, although the cat was half-toned because I used a grey wash in the background. In fact, sometimes it is very effective to half-tone a line drawing on purpose, just for the soft look it produces. This is a very useful ploy when drawing plants and flowers or indeed anything of a delicate nature.

6 TYPES AND STYLES OF ARTWORK

Today there are so many different styles of artwork (largely due to the vast selection of equipment and materials now available in the shops) that it may be a bit daunting to the beginner. In fact some artists prefer to adopt a certain style and stay with it, although it may restrict their scope a little. This probably means they will become recognised by that style and be commissioned accordingly. Whether this is what you choose to do or not is up to you, of course, but whatever you decide to do the next few pages will illustrate the types of artwork you may encounter and therefore perhaps help you to decide.

Natural History

This is a delightful field to specialise in as there are always books being published on some aspect of this ever-popular subject, although be warned that there are a lot of artists already working here. If you do decide to go into this work, the one great requirement will be accuracy in both line and colour. For instance, it would be no good to be asked to do the advertising artwork for the Fox Organisation in which a fox was required as the logo if you were not able to produce a good representation of a fox. It is one thing to get work . . . it is another to be able to do it.

In this field bear in mind, too, that there are a great many highly knowledgeable people who would very soon spot any errors in your work – and you can do without that. One of the great joys of working in this area is that a lot of the time you can work straight from nature. You may not have to consult your reference section at all. Another nice thing about this subject is that it doesn't 'date'; the drawings you do now will be accurate and useful in a hundred years' time. As in every type of artwork you must choose the materials that are going to give you the nearest representation to the natural object.

This is a page for a natural history book showing the designs and shapes found in plants. It goes without saying that the drawing of these items needed to be accurate, clear and precise if they were going to do the job for which they were intended. A vague sketchy approach would not have got the message across.

More natural history . . .

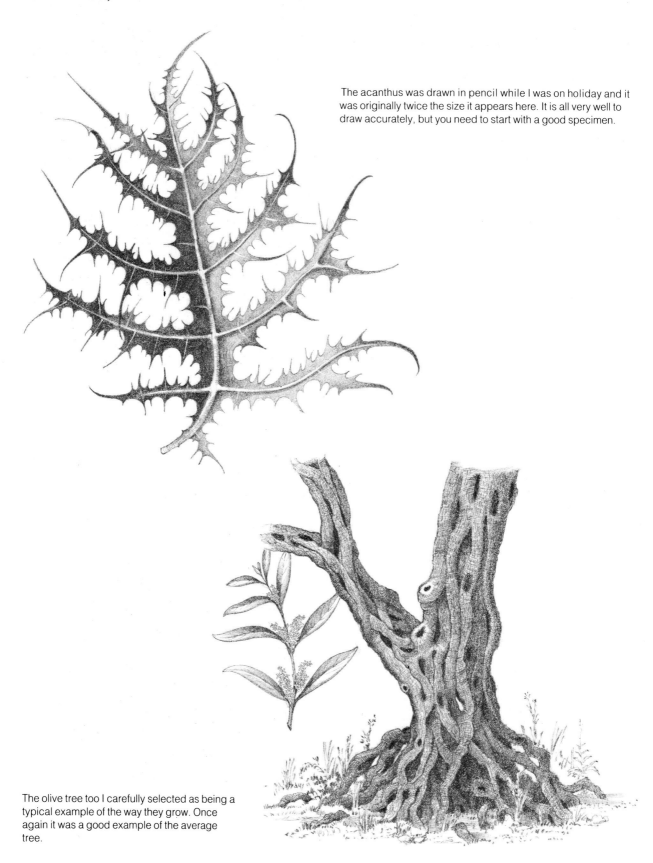

The acanthus was drawn in pencil while I was on holiday and it was originally twice the size it appears here. It is all very well to draw accurately, but you need to start with a good specimen.

The olive tree too I carefully selected as being a typical example of the way they grow. Once again it was a good example of the average tree.

Informative Artwork

This sort of work has to be accurate too. In many ways it is the same sort of 'eye for accuracy' that is needed here as is needed in natural history artwork. In this particular category it is sometimes not so essential to present a realistic piece of artwork as to get the information across. Hence the style employed is often stylised or simplified so that the essential point of the drawing is more pronounced. There are many ways of doing this – the drawing may be diagrammatical (as in the oil drilling diagram) or it may consist of simple line drawings, clearly illustrating the subject concerned (as the page of pen drawings shows), or you may think the style shown on the page from *Purnell's First Dictionary of Science* is the most suitable.

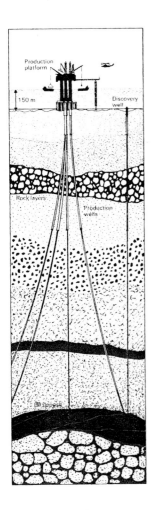

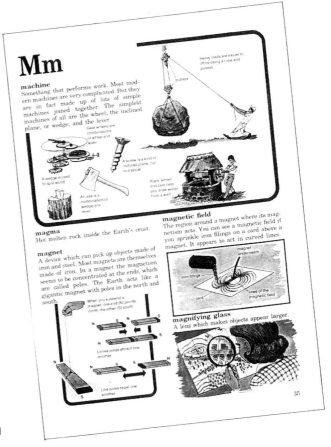

Artwork meant as a means of conveying information must first and foremost do just that. It usually means a clear and uncluttered style is best and perhaps a bit simplified too.

Illustrations under this heading can also become highly skilful works of art in their own right by specialists in their own field. The airbrush work shown here is an example of this sort of informative illustration, combining precision and detail and producing a 'newer than new' look about it.

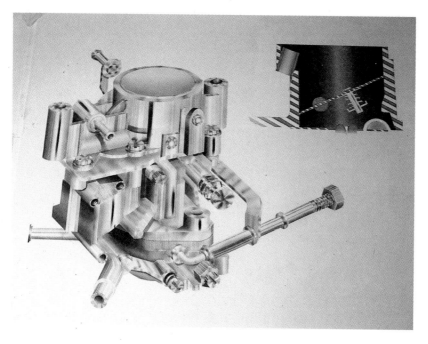

This is a field that the airbrush does very well. The artist is able to portray the smooth shiny surfaces of metal, plastic and glass with particular clarity. It would be difficult to arrive at the same illusion in any other way.

Children's Illustrations

This is the subject that everybody seems to love, and yet it is restricted almost entirely to book illustration and cards. Apart from these two sources of work, there seems to be only children's point-of-sale notices, cards, posters etc (including packaging), and entertainment, which means animation for films and puppets, backgrounds, titles etc, and pantomime.

Most artists at some time or other have a go at children's illustrations – even if only for fun. It normally needs a particular approach in that it wants to be appealing visually as well as having some good ideas behind it – this is the great virtue in children's illustrations.

Generally speaking, all children's drawings and lettering need to be clean, clear and colourful, which is why the favourite style of artwork for children is 'line and wash', in which a simple style outline drawing is made first and then filled in with colour. In practice this usually means the drawing is made in waterproof ink of some sort, or even pencil, and then the areas are filled in with watercolour, which being transparent does not obliterate the drawing. This system seems to fulfil the requirements of children's illustrating in the easiest possible way, coupled with a most attractive result. This has long been the traditional way as well as still being favourite, but nevertheless naturally is not the only way. The style you choose to illustrate a particular story/product/card with is up to you, but it will add greatly to your success if you adopt a style that helps create the atmosphere of the story. Always bear in mind that a great many books are sold almost entirely on the title and jacket, and so the right choice of style of artwork is crucial. In children's work, coloured pencils are used a great deal today with very great success. In fact, some of the best-selling children's books are drawn and coloured in this way.

The potential in the juvenile market is vast, due mainly to the modern printing techniques that have made full colour books, and general printing too, such a viable proposition. Once the die is cast, competition takes over and the whole thing snowballs, which is good news for the artist. But, despite this plethora of work and opportunity, once again be warned – there are a lot of artists working in this field and so the actual amount of work that one artist gets may not be a lot. Nevertheless if you think you have a real feeling for children's work (not just copying Disney characters) then go to it!

I think there is little to say about these characters, they are purely for visual enjoyment.

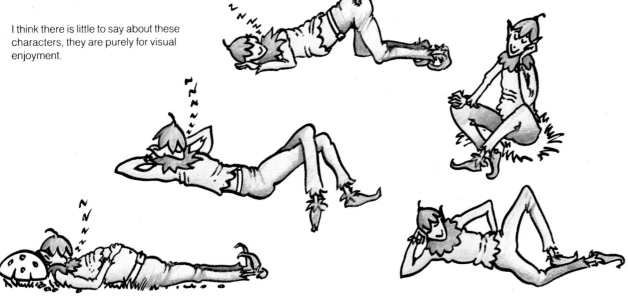

This children's Christmas card shows how a mechanical tint can be used simply and how it helps the drawing to complete the shapes.

This is a pencil drawing of a roe deer. Pencil is a good medium to used for animals because it is easy to express the softness of their coats of fur. Can I remind you again – it is not only the skill of your drawing that will get you noticed but the thinking behind the drawing. How much more attractive this deer is because it is looking up rather than just standing in an inanimate pose. Animation is the key word.

they peered in through the little doorway

This first sketch for an illustration in a children's book was done with a ballpoint pen. They can be used in the same way as a pencil to achieve lines of varying denseness.

Mechanical Tints

This is an aid to artwork (mainly black and white) rather than a type, although it does almost produce a style of its own. Most people are familiar with the range of textures and tones that are available, although the significance of their use is not always appreciated, i.e. that it allows a 'line' drawing to have a tonal range whilst retaining the crispness of line work that is so attractive. The reason for this is that the mechanical tint is made up of a series of lines/dots/circles, or whatever, which are all solid line and not vignetted, just as if you had drawn them by hand with a pen. All these tints come in sheets – some as the rub-down transfer type and some as transparent sheets with a low-tack adhesive backing. In the case of the latter the area to be tinted is cut from the sheet with a stencil knife and laid in position on the artwork. There are advantages and disadvantages with both systems, and so as usual you must try them both and decide which you can use the best.

Perhaps this is a good moment to make a point about black and white artwork in general. The reason why a mechanical tint reproduces so well is because of its denseness and sharpness (its blackness). Incidentally, the same may be said of scraperboard work – even the very finest of lines reproduces faithfully, for the same reason. And so, when doing your ordinary black and white artwork (if it is for reproduction), do endeavour to make the lines a dense black, and see that the work is done on good bright white paper. It is very easy to say that it doesn't matter a lot because these days our modern printing equipment will cope with any condition of artwork. Well, in some ways it can, but you will still get better results if your work is a good solid black on a good bright white.

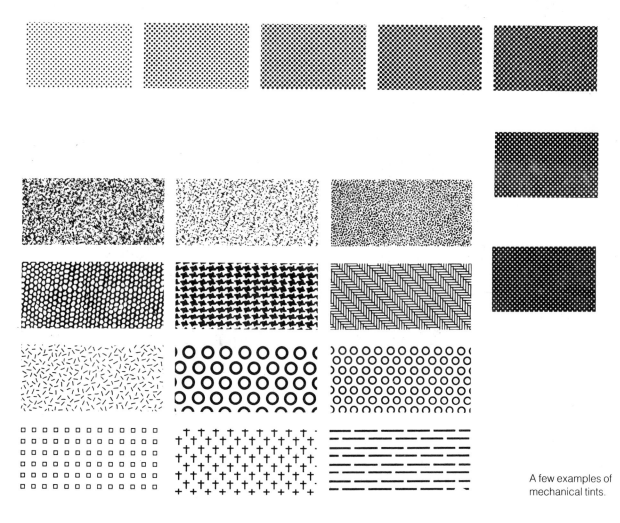

A few examples of mechanical tints.

This is another example of the use of mechanical tints; it is also an example of stylised artwork. In fact the two work very well together because in some respects the tinting could be considered stylised toning. This sort of illustration reproduces very well as it is a 'line' process with the added advantage of at least one other tone and often more.

Stylised Artwork

This is where the artist provides perhaps rather more style than accuracy. The result is a sort of 'enhancing' of the subject, but it must be done with a great deal of care and a lot of thought beforehand. It is used in promotional work mainly; some artists' work can be recognised by their particular style in the same way that a person's handwriting is recognisable. If you are lucky or clever enough to evolve a good style it may well spell success for you because if customers see your work appearing now and again in this attractive way, they will start asking whose work it is, and your commissions will come to you rather than you having to go looking for them.

One hint about creating a style: it is usually the result of having become extremely adept in one particular medium. Therefore it is probably best to adopt a medium first and then develop it to the limit of your capability.

This sort of treatment works well for this type of subject. However it would not do for everything and that is why the type and style of artwork you use has to be carefully chosen.

More stylised artwork. The reason for this sort of work is that it
makes it 'appropriate' or 'suitable' for a particular use. In the
same way you choose colours and typestyles, so you choose a
style for artwork. Suitability of artwork to its use is the subject of the
next chapter.

Advertising

Advertising comes very high indeed in a commercial artist's life. Everywhere we look we see examples of advertising art, and yet it would be impossible to categorise work in this field because it is spread so wide. 'Almost anything goes' can easily be said about this section where there are apparently no rules and not even any guidelines to offer. However, perhaps the one word that describes what all studios working in this area want most of all is 'ideas'. If you are able to come up with a steady stream of ideas, good practical ideas that is, then you should consider the varied and interesting world of advertising.

One characteristic type of work employed in advertising more than anywhere else is the exaggerated or distorted look. Everyone is familiar with the extra tall and thin drawings of fashion models used to advertise everything from the elegant clothes they wear to the motor cars they drape themselves over. The cars also are often depicted as being extra wide, or extra low, or

super luxurious – all as a result of the way they are illustrated. Likewise exaggerated perspective is another common ploy used to practically the same effect.

All this can lead to very creative artwork, which can be exciting to do for its own sake, because often it requires quite original thinking at the outset, so once again it is ideas that count.

The ideas that are so important to the designer are just as important to the copy-writer. New products and new materials will always need new presentations and new styling. This means you have to get your timing right, which means making sure that the new 'angle' is ready for the customer just when he needs it to coincide with a new campaign. Actually as you go on experimenting with your drawing and designing you will begin to 'pigeon-hole' your work subconsciously; you will start thinking to yourself 'now this would be a good way to advertise so and so'. When you reach that stage you will start being very useful as a commercial artist.

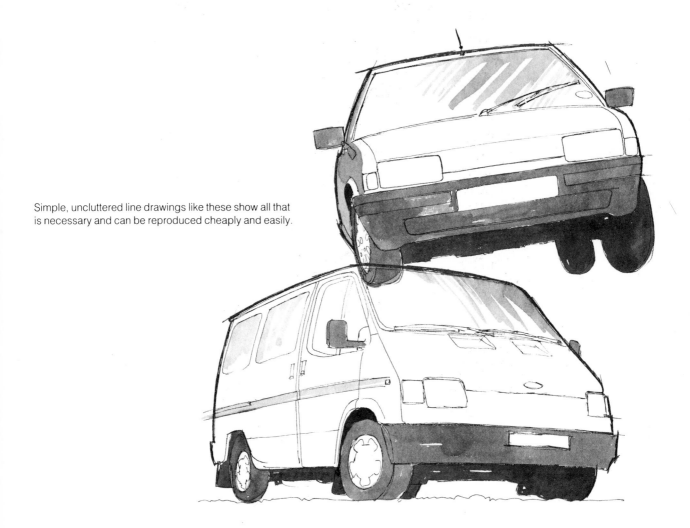

Simple, uncluttered line drawings like these show all that is necessary and can be reproduced cheaply and easily.

HEADS UP!
Look Before You Cross

Adjust to changing weather conditions

VISIBILITY POOR
BE SEEN

SAFE SPEEDS
may become **TOO FAST**

GIVE A DIM!
BE FIRST TO LOWER BEAMS

Safe Walking Demands **EXTRA CARE** in **BAD WEATHER**

FOG RAIN SNOW
KEEP HEADLIGHTS ON LOW

SEE YELLOW?
be prepared to **STOP!**

take your life in your own hands
BUCKLE UP!

you can't be recycled
BUCKLE UP!

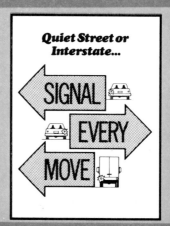

Quiet Street or Interstate...
SIGNAL EVERY MOVE

AT NIGHT...
reflect light!

A GOOD BELT FOR THE ROAD

PLAY IT SAFE
ON THE JOB
ON VACATION

before you go- **CHECK YOUR TOW**
✓LIGHTS ✓HITCH ✓BRAKES
✓TURN SIGNALS ✓MIRRORS

BEHIND THE WHEEL
When you're three sheets to the wind...
You don't stand a ghost of a chance

7 SUITABILITY OF THE ARTWORK TO ITS USE

I have mentioned this important point before and I do not hesitate to do so again. The suitability of a design or drawing to its use is so important. It is not necessarily a criticism of the skill or talents of the artist if the customer decides it isn't quite right; it is quite likely to be a poor choice of approach. Perhaps 'unsuitability' is found more in connection with the reproduction process that is going to be used – customers are generally hazy about this subject anyway, and so it would be very sensible of you to get yourself thoroughly acquainted with those processes as soon as you can, because it will be largely up to you as the designer/artist to give guidance on the subject. The customer will almost certainly look to you for helpful suggestions and professional tips in this matter, and of course you will have to produce the artwork suitable for that sort of reproduction or else the printer also will not be at all happy with you.

To give a simple example: it would be no good producing a superb pencil drawing if the request was for a 'line' drawing. Likewise it would be senseless to produce an intricate design using a great many colours and a lot of shading for a shop facia to be cut out in acrylic sheet, when the job would be much better suited

Practise with all the materials you can. You will find you get on with some better than others.

soft pencil

fibre tip pen (waterproof)

dip pen indian ink (waterproof)

stylo pen (waterproof)

brush - poster colour.

coloured pencil

to a signwriter. Finally, it wouldn't be very professional to design a large and prestigious site board for a firm of contractors who were developing a building site, if it was over the size limit imposed by the local planning authority, or if the lettering you depicted was larger than that allowed in the area.

A typical example of how useful a photograph can be in helping to produce a visual for either the customer or Local Authority.

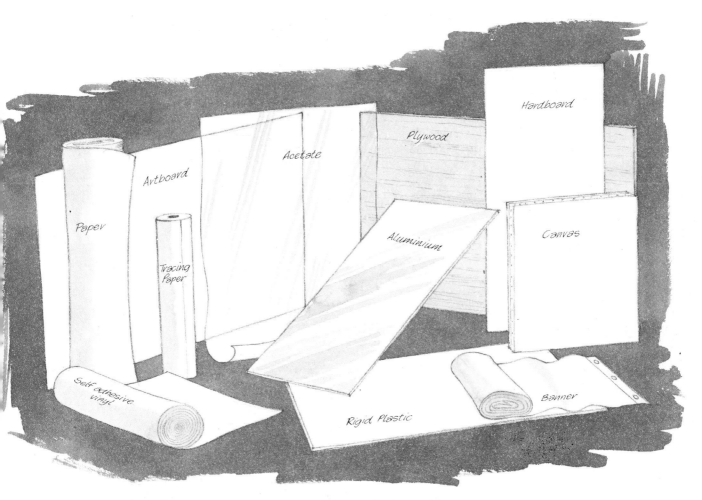

Not only must we be greatly concerned with the materials we are going to work with but the grades, thicknesses, textures and finishes must also be understood and appreciated if we are to advise customers in a professional capacity. What is more, new materials and products are constantly appearing on the market which means it is increasingly difficult to keep up with the situation. No one will expect you to keep a stock of all the materials you might use, but you should know where to obtain a product when you need it.

So 'suitability' is of great concern at the graphic stage, but it is also just as important when it comes to choosing the materials to do the job with. This means designing to their limitation and yet for their potential. The variety of materials now available for displays/signs/exhibitions/general illustration etc is almost matched by the selection of paints/inks/lacquers/varnishes/fixatives etc to put on them. The reason for such choice is that all materials have become so specialised and complicated in their production that to use the wrong materials together (the wrong paint on acrylic for instance) might well spell disaster. First of all, then, make your choice of material, be it vinyl, aluminium, hardboard, plywood, glass, nylon, polythene or whatever (the most suitable for the job) and then make sure you do the work on it with the right product. Read up all the literature on products that you can get your hands on until you are thoroughly familiar with them.

This is an extemely good moment for me quietly to remind you that the customer very seldom knows exactly what he wants, and even when he thinks he does it is not often the best choice in the world, because he can't be expected to know as much as you do about your own job. It is therefore up to you to be on top of your subject and to restrain him firmly from an unwise decision; he will thank you for it eventually and think more of you anyway.

The next consideration must be the brushes, pens, pencils, erasers, compasses etc; what we call the 'hand tools'. Suitability is essential: you wouldn't dream of painting a signboard with a watercolour brush or painting a portrait with a gilding brush; you would never be able to get a professional finish to it, and it would be immensely difficult trying to! Take a look round your nearest art shop and examine the range of tools in stock, make sure you understand what they are all for, and ask yourself if you are adequately equipped to do the work you are doing to the very best of your ability. In other words, are your tools handicapping you? It pays to do this regularly; have a look round, keep up to date, and don't get left behind.

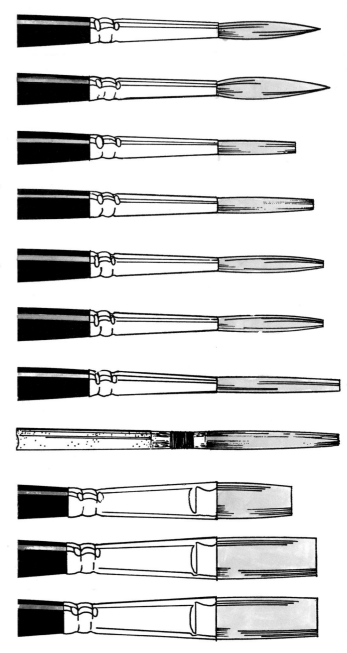

Above is a selection of signwriting brushes; pointed, chisel and flat. The handles are usually colour coded to help in their selection and recognition.

The brush on the left is actual size and is very good for filling in large areas, whether enamel on signs or water colour backgrounds.

A 'chinagraph' pencil is always useful to have around. It writes on all shiny surfaces and yet is water soluble.

A putty rubber can be moulded into shapes for cleaning detailed artwork.

When using poster colours always try to use a water-proof variety; it gives peace of mind.

The kind of paper you use makes all the difference to the end result. Look at the comparison between rough and smooth surfaces.

Some things are not suitable ....

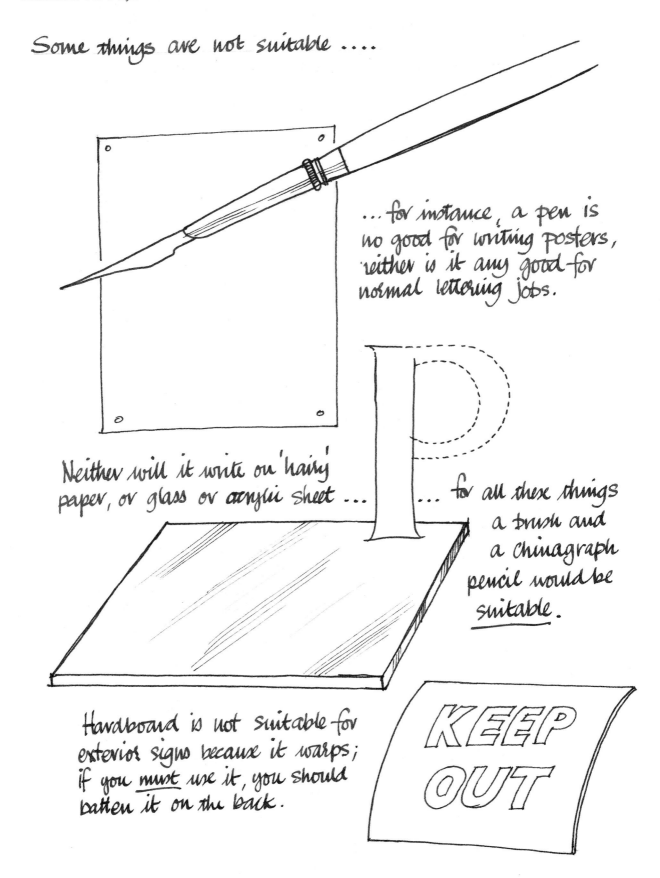

... for instance, a pen is no good for writing posters, neither is it any good for normal lettering jobs.

Neither will it write on 'hairy' paper, or glass or acrylic sheet ...

... for all these things a brush and a chinagraph pencil would be suitable.

Hardboard is not suitable for exterior signs because it warps; if you <u>must</u> use it, you should batten it on the back.

KEEP OUT

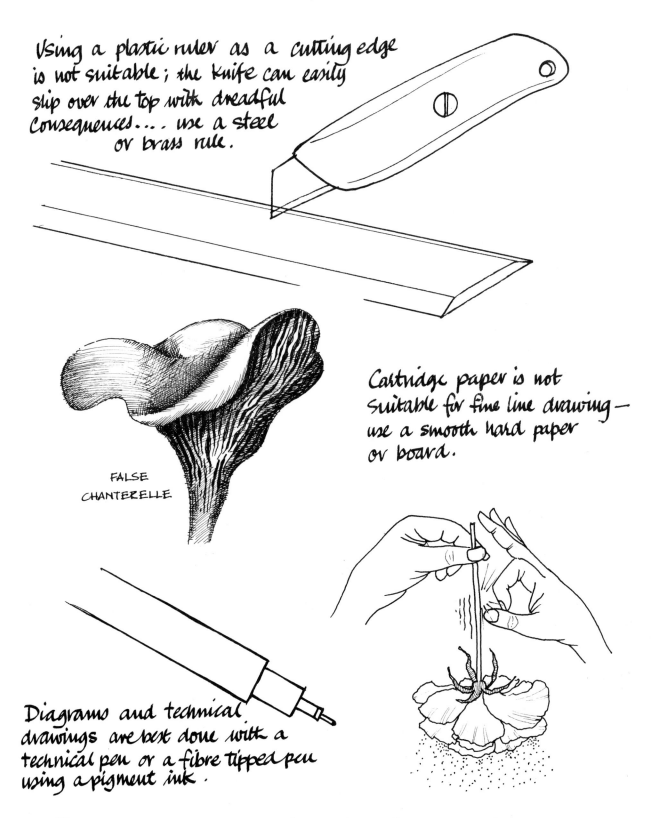

Using a plastic ruler as a cutting edge is not suitable; the knife can easily slip over the top with dreadful consequences.... use a steel or brass rule.

Cartridge paper is not suitable for fine line drawing — use a smooth hard paper or board.

FALSE CHANTERELLE

Diagrams and technical drawings are best done with a technical pen or a fibre tipped pen using a pigment ink.

Remember — the most suitable equipment always works best.

8 BOOK ILLUSTRATION

If book illustrating is your great desire, there are three ways you can go about it. First you can approach a publisher direct with samples of your work and a request for a chance to show what you can do. This is not a very good method for all sorts of reasons, although it does sometimes come off. When you are desperate it is surprising what you can do. If you do adopt this approach, a good tip is that art editors are very human and try to avoid trouble, so you will stand a much greater chance of getting work from them if your attitude is pleasant and you get on well together.

The second approach is by way of an author. If you happen to know of an author, then try approaching him personally. Authors often have to commission their own artists, so this could lead to something fruitful. First of all you must get some work done; any author or art editor will certainly want to see samples of your work, and they will have to be suitable (remember?). In this case it means suitable either for the publishing house you approach or the particular work that an author is engaged on at the time.

The third way is through an agent. Some people have pretty strong things to say about agents, but circumstances play a very big part in colouring this viewpoint. If you do decide to enrol with an agency, do make your choice carefully because they differ greatly in the type of work they get and the standard they require. Make sure the one you choose is going to be able to get commissions for *your sort* of work. It is not a bit of good going to an agent because he handles large influential clients if the work he gets from them is not your style or the finish they require is above that which you can deliver. All you will get out of it is a lot of worry, because you will only get paid 'on receipt of acceptable artwork'.

This was a little illustration I did in line and wash for a book on black magic. I think everybody has worked in line and wash at some time or other and it is very suitable for reproduction.

An agent will take a percentage of the earnings you receive from the work they introduce you to, which is not as bad as it sounds when you consider that they will probably have negotiated a better deal for you with the publisher or client than you would have done for yourself. And they do know the most likely clients to sell your work to.

I don't think you should raise your hopes too quickly, however, whichever method you adopt (you might try all three at the same time), because there are many disappointments, cancellations and 'putting backs' along the way which become very frustrating to the artist as there is nothing he can do about it.

Having made contact with your publisher, the editor or art editor will brief you as to what it is they want. They will tell you, for instance, how many illustrations they want, what type (black and white, or colour, or a number of each), they might go as far as to tell you what

style of work they are looking for. They will also most likely have a preference as to the size they are drawn. It is quite common to have them drawn larger than the final printed size (a word about that in a moment). One of the good things about book illustration is that the fee and the working schedule is arranged at the beginning; this obviates some of the embarrassment and misunderstanding that can otherwise occur later on. The fee incidentally is usually paid in two or three instalments, either half on signing the contract and half on delivery 'of acceptable artwork', or one-third on signing the contract, one-third on delivery, and one-third on publication.

As artwork for books is obviously all for reproduction, a look at the types of work required for the various printing processes, and the scale at which they are submitted, will prove useful.

This is the easy way to proportionally enlarge or reduce all right-angled formats.

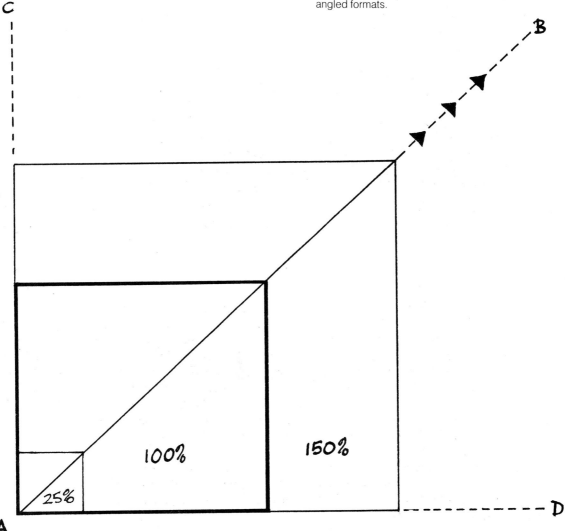

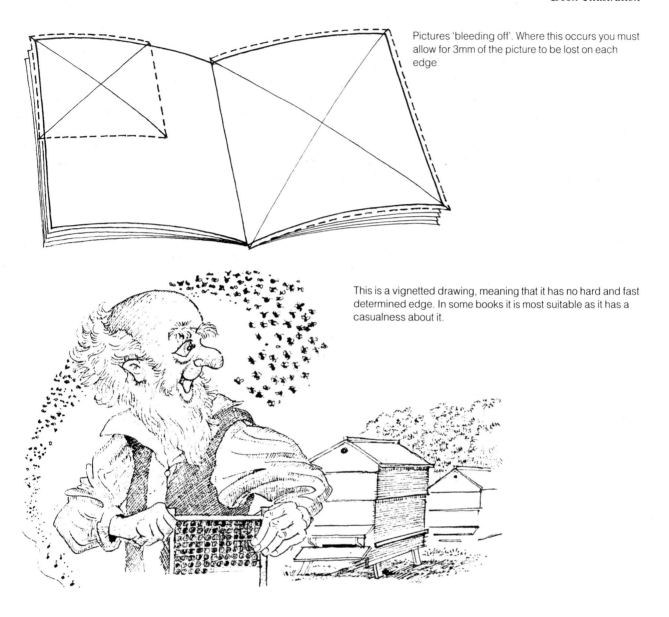

Pictures 'bleeding off'. Where this occurs you must allow for 3mm of the picture to be lost on each edge.

This is a vignetted drawing, meaning that it has no hard and fast determined edge. In some books it is most suitable as it has a casualness about it.

Scale and Arrangement on the Page

The size at which you do your work is sometimes important to the publishers. They often like to commission their work a little larger than finished size because they feel it 'tightens up' by reducing the errors and sharpening the line. The percentage of the enlarged artwork is fairly well defined as well; it is usual to present it at either 125 per cent or 150 per cent, that is either one-quarter larger than the finished size or one-half larger than the finished size. To work for a larger reduction than this starts to present one or two problems as far as the artist is concerned; mainly that he has to judge very carefully how he does his work so that when the reduction is finally made nothing is lost in the artwork.

The arrangement on the page is important, too, although this is mainly the province of the book designer. Illustrations can be 'squared off' or boxed in, which is the most usual way, but sometimes it suits the style of picture or the type of book to have them vignetted, that is with no definitive edges. In this case they normally take the vague shape of an oval, but with the edges gradually fading out. Alternatively the picture could 'bleed off', which means it goes off the edge of the page on one or more sides.

These considerations may seem a little trivial on the face of it, but it actually is quite necessary to establish them at the outset because they often affect the composition of the drawing.

Stories

Whether fiction or non-fiction, here the approach is quite different. Apart from the decision as to what will be colour and what will be black and white, the style of illustration is all-important. The reason why some of our great illustrators are great is because they are able to create the right atmosphere for the story by the very way they do their illustrations. For instance, *The Wind in the Willows* (Kenneth Grahame) has over the years been illustrated by a number of artists, but strangely enough none have been more in keeping with the general atmosphere of the book than the originals by E.H. (Kipper) Shepard. The same can be said of *Winnie the Pooh* (A.A. Milne), where the drawings 'took over the page'. In fact these stories (and others) have become such favourites to a large extent because of the illustrator's skill. To take the point to the ultimate, some books are collected just because of the pictures.

So the point about getting the style exactly right is most critical.

As I said earlier, artwork for the children's market is a great attraction for everybody, and all that I have just said can apply equally well to the children's market. The materials you use are nothing like as important as the way you use them. A great deal depends on the age group you are working for (something the publisher will make quite clear) so, apart from the very young who will be attracted by bold colours and shapes, the other age groups will certainly be starting to think, and that means they will be beginning to be discerning about what they read and what pictures they like. Make your illustrations tell more than the essentials – make the characters overact slightly so that they come off the page to children as *real*. It doesn't matter at all how simple the drawings are as long as they are appealing and alive, moving and real!

This is a pencil and wash drawing – another favourite combination. Nearly all artwork is set out in pencil to start with but it remains to be decided whether you intend to leave the pencil showing on the finished artwork or whether your painting disguises it.

This was a drawing for a children's book of pets. It was done with a
charcoal pencil and a little watercolour. It is the naturalness of the
pose and the composition that is important and must be right
before you attempt to start a finished drawing.

The illustration above is a charcoal drawing with a wash of grey watercolour which means for reproduction it has to half-toned. This was for a book *Stories of Jesus*. The other two illustrations on this page are line drawings and were done with a stylo pen.

Informative or Method Illustration

Informative illustrations are used in all types of practical books from art and craft to car maintenance and horse-riding. Accepting the theory that one picture is worth a thousand words, these books use a great number of instructional and method drawings. Generally speaking, this sort of illustration is kept to a simple uncluttered outline drawing, presenting a clear and factual graphic statement. In this way it really can convey a great deal of information in one illustration. Indeed, sometimes when it is difficult to explain a situation in words a drawing may be the only way.

Captions can help a lot. A caption is a sentence or two that usually goes close under the picture to explain in words what is going on. These captions are usually set in a smaller typeface than the body text, and sometimes in a different style. There is also 'labelling'. When a particular detail in a picture is referred to it is sometimes better to label it as shown.

In more complicated subjects the problem of showing detail is overcome by cut-away drawings or 'exploded' drawings. Either of these methods is normally the job of a specialist artist since it requires the use of equipment that would otherwise be seldom used. The less complicated way is to magnify certain areas so that labels can be applied.

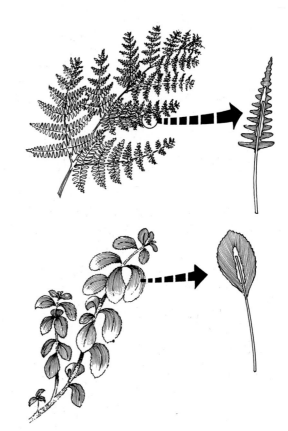

These were also drawn with stylo pen which is ideal for this type of illustration. One advantage of working with waterproof ink is that corrections can be made with process white which doesn't mix with the ink and make a horrible mess.

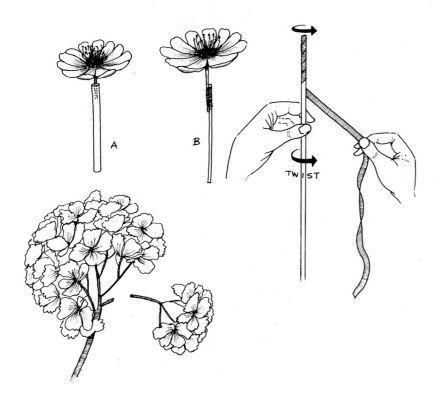

When you investigate this market for the first time, remember some publishers are more orientated to the children's market than others, so it will pay you to choose carefully before you start spending time writing and sending samples of your work.

This brings us to the subject of sending work. The publishers will not be responsible for anything you might send them, and, although it is highly unlikely they will damage or lose anything while it is in their hands, you have to make sure it gets to them safely to start with. Therefore I think it is unwise to entrust original artwork to the normal postal service. If at all possible it is better to give up the time and deliver it yourself, but failing that either send it by registered post or by some form of security delivery service. Do

These two illustrations are watercolour and pencil combined. I'm sure everybody has used this method but nonetheless it is very effective and suitable way of going about a lot of work.

take copies of your work before you part with it – you will be surprised how useful this can be even just to have it in front of you when discussing it on the telephone.

Here are a few tips about the presentation of your work. Give all artwork a flap-over overlay to protect it. Mark on the actual artwork the reduction it is drawn for and also mark which is the TOP. If the work is in colour make sure you do it on paper (not board) because it has to be placed on a cylinder for scanning during the separation process. If you do make a mistake or forget, and you do do it on board, either you or the printer will have to peel off the paper from the support board before it can be used.

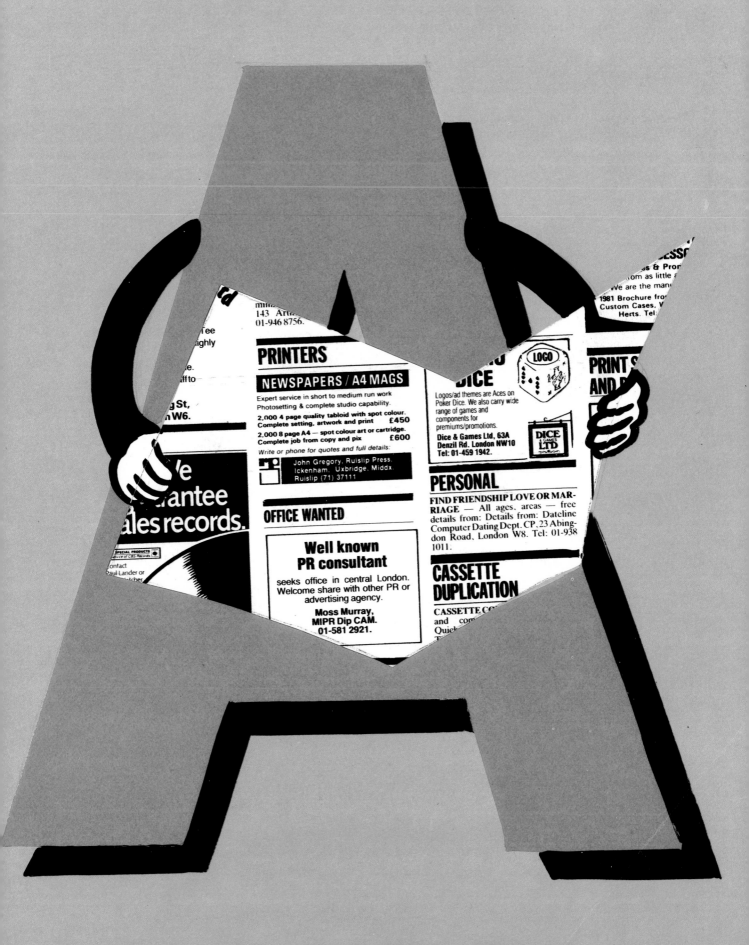

9 ADVERTISING

This is the field where most commercial artists spend most of their time. Not only is this a vast market, but like lettering it is an essential one. Everybody (almost) needs to advertise, from the self-employed painter and decorator to the giants of industry. The only real difference is the money they spend on their advertising.

If you have a real talent for coming up with original ideas or new approaches to the way things are presented, then you should certainly try to get into advertising. All advertising carries a message, sometimes blatantly obvious and sometimes very subtle, but however it is done it is the idea that counts.

A page of small ads from a trade magazine. It is always a good idea to look at the surrounding ads on a page before starting on your own.

Posters really do come in all sizes and colours and almost everybody has written a poster in their time, even if it was only for the church bazaar. However, producing posters for billposting companies to use on hoardings for instance is quite a different proposition – they even have to be folded in the right order

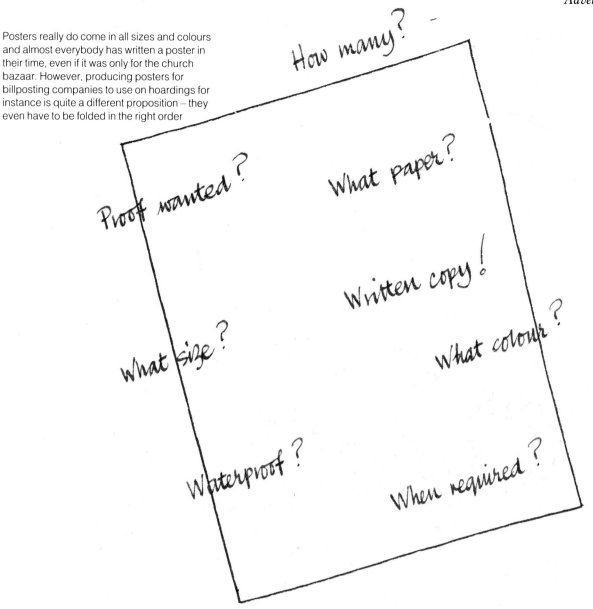

Posters

Posters are the simplest way of getting a message around to the public. They are used by the vicar to advertise the village jumble sale and by politicians to advertise their party, so there is a place for the commercial artist to work at all levels. However, there are always the same questions to be answered no matter what the level of work.

1) What size will the poster be? (Make it an economic paper size.)
2) How many are required? This will tell you how it is to be produced – either by hand or printed.
3) How many colours? If there are only a few posters to be done by hand, it doesn't really matter much about the number of colours.

4) What type of paper? For instance, there is a lot of difference in cost between a plain white MG (machine-grained) and a fluorescent paper.
5) Are they going to be used inside or outside? If they are for outside use you will have to use waterproof poster paint.
6) What are the details? Do insist on the 'copy' in writing to ensure that you get it right. And if you come across a dubious spelling in the copy, get the dictionary out and check it, because customers' spelling can be very curious at times!

A word in general about posters: do try to get some design quality into them even if they are only for the village jumble sale – you will get no satisfaction from your work if you don't.

Newspapers and Magazines

Along with posters as a source of work for a 'jobbing' commercial artist, there must also come general printing and advertising layout and design for newspapers and magazines. The scope is just as wide as for posters, since there is work to be done for the local weekly paper just as well as for national magazines. At present most of the newspaper ads are in black and white, of course, whereas there is a good chance of a colour commission for a national 'glossy' magazine, and some of them even rely on freelance work for their covers.

Send your card in to the local paper for the attention of the art editor, with a note explaining what you can do and the service you can give. Next time he is in need of some 'outwork' he may well remember you – and then it's up to you!

Dry transfer lettering, or rub down lettering has become a generally accepted method of producing instant lettering. A number of manufacturers are now producing it in small sheets as well as the full sheets which we are familiar with. The range too is increasing.

As with posters, there is a strong element of lettering in most small ads, and so it is fairly essential that you have some form of instant lettering available. This will not be the same sort of lettering you are using for posters, incidentally. Lettering in general is discussed in Chapter 11, but since we have to mention it here in connection with advertising I have to point out that there is a different approach to lettering in the two cases. In this context (small ads) the sort of lettering will probably be either the dry transfer type or photoset. In both cases the resultant artwork will be a paste-up.

The particular advertisement you are concerned with should fit in to the type/style/class of publication it is going in – the art editor will have something to say about that. You will need to know the column width (ads are taken as multiples of a column), or the part of a page the advertiser has bought. The measures are very accurate and you will have to work accordingly. The other important item is the schedule. If 'camera-ready' artwork has to be in by noon on Thursday, then that must be your deadline. If you are ill, or make a mistake, or lose the copy, that is your problem; the advertisement must still be in on time.

You can see here the arrangements of space for advertisements.

Other Advertising Areas

Among the other advertising areas in general advertising (excluding film and television, which is another subject entirely) there are signs, brochures, leaflets, handbills, banners, exhibitions and shows, trade fairs and point of sale displays. The exhibitions, shows and trade fairs are all construction jobs in their initial stages and therefore the province of tradesmen such as carpenters. The commercial artist is then asked to supply his work on panelling for fixing to the general construction.

These events are normally advertised themselves long beforehand, giving the exhibition secretary's telephone number; send your card along as soon as you can – there is a lot of work for a commercial artist in setting up an exhibition.

The next few pages show some ideas and examples of the types of artwork and approach that can be used to effect, along with some slogans and phrases.

Figures

Undoubtedly the single most useful asset a commercial artist can have is the ability to draw good figures. If you cannot draw your own figures, it is better to get someone else to draw them for you rather than spoil your work; some artists specialise in drawing figures in the same way that others specialise in cars or trees. If, however, you *can* draw figures, do use them as much as you can, because they almost always improve a layout – rather like a swan improves water or cows improve a meadow.

These are all pen drawings but they would have worked just as well in either pencil or brush. The main thing is they should look right in the advertisement.

The heads were dry brushed with black poster paint and the hands were drawn with a charcoal pencil onto a rough watercolour paper; both have been reduced from the original.

Heads and Hands Too!

When there is no room for a full figure, a head may do just as well, especially if it can be given an expression suitable to the situation. In most cases a nice attractive smile is all that is necessary to provide the 'life' in the layout that is so friendly. This is where practising with cartoons is so helpful, because the principles of expression are just the same. Try drawing the same head over and over again giving it a different expression each time – surprise, astonishment, happiness and concentration are the most useful ones.

Hands on their own can be equally helpful in producing an interesting layout. They are constantly needed to point or hold in a multitude of situations in every sphere of advertising. In fact, in a lot of cases, the particular way in which the hand is doing something is in itself a valuable instruction on the way to do it; back to a picture being worth a thousand words! Don't forget when drawing hands to use the correct one, i.e. male or female; and another point to consider is whether the person should be right- or left-handed – it can make a lot of difference if it is a method drawing.

Not only adults but children too . . .

The first two children were drawn to the never-failing formula of large doe eyes and small snub noses . . .

the other two are less cartoonish but they were all ideal for the job they were intended for.

All shapes and sizes.

Figures are not always adult, of course; children also need to be practised – boys and girls of all ages, shapes and types. Get a typical family of figures together in your reference box, ready for when they are needed, because they will be a great help in holiday brochures or new car advertisements. The children are especially helpful because in the right circumstances they can be drawn to overact beautifully and in consequence highlight the mood of the ad. These sorts of drawings can say so much more about the atmosphere than any photographic or representational drawing can do. You should cast your eye around for good examples of figures, heads and hands in advertising and study how they are done. This brings me to a very important point: are you able to distinguish between good and mediocre examples? If you can confidently say that you can, then there is no more to be said and you will be able to set your own standards with no trouble. If on the other hand you find it difficult to decide, then I suggest you confine your attentions to national advertising rather than local publicity. The reason is not that local work is in any way unprofessional but rather that with national campaigns you are almost guaranteed a fairly high standard. If you are going to look at other artists' work as a guide to your own, you owe it to yourself to be influenced only by the best – why copy mediocre work when there is so much good stuff about?

It is ideas that count in advertising, so how about this for the film
'The Invisible Man'? Its virtue lies in the fact that it is bold and
simple and would reproduce easily by any process.

'Sleep soundly tonight with the Secure Insurance Co'. Another animal ad that is always a safe bet with the public.

For a good meal, try Joe's.

Animals

Animals, especially pets, are stars every time. We are all aware of the TV ads where puppies and kittens are the main characters and steal the show; and they are obviously very successful, otherwise they would not have been such long-lasting favourites. The way you actually draw your animals will depend a lot on the customer and/or the advertising agency that commissions you. To repeat a point I made earlier, it is not the materials you use in your work but the way you use them; get as much out of every line you draw as you possibly can.

Sometimes even unlikely animals like my giraffe seem to be exactly right, and therefore serve as a reminder to keep all good drawings and photographs in your reference box. One day just the right occasion will come along when you need that unusual reference.

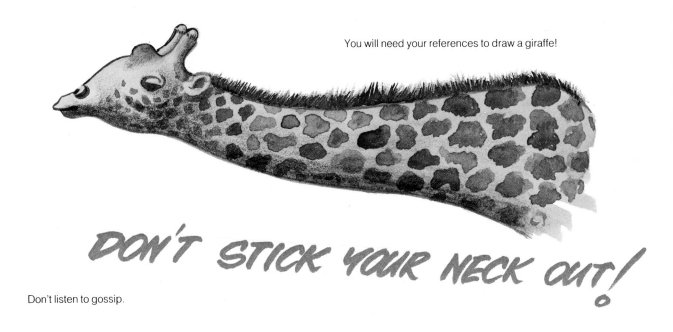

You will need your references to draw a giraffe!

Don't listen to gossip.

It's ideas that count – even in the simple jobs . . .

112

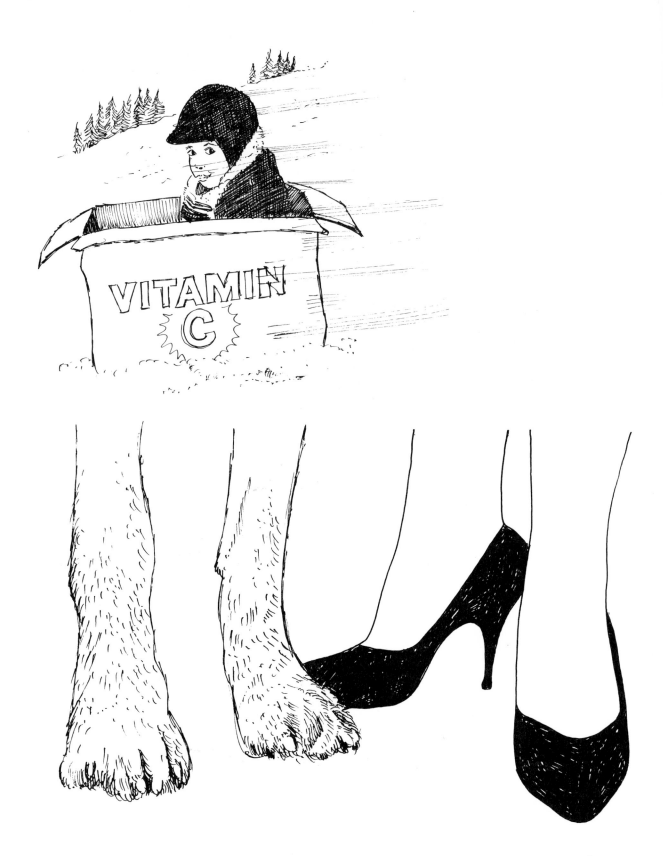

WHATEVER THE TREATMENT.... A QUARTEX FLOOR WILL TAKE IT !

YOU NEED A PAINT THAT LASTS !

Recognised colour matching systems usually come in handy
packs or sheets.

When matching your colours (or choosing them) do take them into
the daylight. Fluorescent tubes and some other types of lighting
are notorious for altering the visual conception of colour. Also, the
same recipe for a colour may look quite different on another type
of surface; it can also look quite different as a gloss finish from that
of a matt finish.

Catalogues and books of typefaces should be able to be laid open flat.

You can never have too many of these books because one book never has all the typefaces. You will often have to lend one to a customer anyway. As well as printers' typefaces, look out for the more free-style lettering books like the one on the next page.

Snaps!

Just a gentle touch tunes
your auto radio electronically...

. heat automatically...

The Big
Moments
with
Color Shots!

Switch to Tubeless Tire
Safety at No Extra Cost!

HICKORY

An Extra Richness !

Fresh!

2 ounces in each serving supply more
of milk's vital food values than
a big 8 oz glass of milk -

Golden and Glowing
with Velvet...

Wake up ... Beautiful
Color on Your Lips

The Champagne of bottled products

LILAC

Fashionable "alive" Masters

91

You will not find these alphabets in a printer's list or as a rub down
letter: however they will give you more ideas for handlettering.

Cartoons

Cartoons always have a special appeal, and often a good cartoon character can become as well-known as the product it promotes. Cartoons have more character than realistic drawings and can be more outrageous in the way they give the message. The advantage with cartoons, as far as the artist is concerned, is that they are quick to draw and easy to reproduce because they are mainly constructed with good bold lines. The most time is taken up with creating a suitable situation or expression to go along with the particular slogan or message that the advertisement is trying to get across. Rather than try to draw a selection of characters, try working on just one; it is better to develop one good 'all-round' character that you can draw easily and quickly, in any mood or position. In that way your cartoons will become slick and smooth – the sign of a real professional – and will start to earn you money. It has often been the case that when an advertising campaign is beginning to lose its way the injection of something like a brand new cartoon character will resurrect the whole thing.

The strange thing about cartoons is that they are classless; they seem to be acceptable in most situations. Cartoon characters are quick to draw and fun to do. If you find yourself in a position where you can't seem to quite get the right style of artwork for the particular job in hand, try it with a cartoon – it sometimes comes out better than the original idea.

It is easy to imagine what these characters could be saying to each other, which would be very difficult to achieve by more representational artwork.

More cartoons and slogans too. If you can supply a good
punchline or slogan to back up your cartoons they will be a lot
more useful. Some on-going campaigns run by large companies
rely entirely for their success on the cartoon and its punchline
appearing regularly.

Try a simple face to experiment with getting expressions without a
lot of complicated lines.

More of the same.

These two characters were used in an advertising campaign by a
firm of printers who were offering a service in good quality
business cards.

This is a rough for a book jacket using cartoon style characters. It is another example of the wide field in which cartoons can be used.

Lettering

No matter how good or important the artwork is, it is nearly always used in association with words, which is lettering as far as the artist is concerned and will have to be considered as part of the overall design of the layout. Lettering, then, not only has to be allowed for when planning a layout but has to be considered in detail, i.e. the position, size and style. The position is probably the easiest of the three to establish, and the size shouldn't really prove to be too much of a decision to make, but the typeface may very well cause some headscratching and opinion-searching.

If it is to be a standard typeface, it can be chosen in the normal way from any catalogue of typefaces, but if it is to be hand lettered you will have to produce rough artwork to show what you propose. Hand lettering is a

Practise putting lettering in and around your artwork. Make the lettering style be descriptive as well as the pictures. Sometimes it looks better to have the lettering as part of the artwork, or running across the front or even behind. Try it all ways before you finally submit the work. Above all be imaginative.

Modern - A B C D E F abca 24

Modern Alphabets Inc 30

Modern Alphabets 36

Modern Alphab 42

Modern Alph 48

Modern A 60

The advantage with a book of typefaces is that they also give you the 'point size' of the character, which enables you once again to be professional in your specifications.

personal achievement and has a certain character about it, rather like handwriting, which makes it is easy to tell from the lettering who it was that did it; this is why you must be very particular about this area of commercial art. It has been said by a great many artists and letterers that there is nothing in the art world that needs such precision as lettering. Well, be that as it may, but it does have one curious quality that every signwriter will be only too aware of, and that is that the errors in lettering become more obvious the further you get away from it (within limitations of course). However, at the moment we are not considering signwriting particularly but general handlettering in artwork for advertising purposes, and under these circumstances there is no point at all in hand lettering a typeface that can be produced from some mechanical or photographic method. Confine yourself therefore to lettering that cannot be produced any other way and that has a very definite personal character.

Lettering is always more interesting if it can be woven into the general layout and become part of the design in its own right. Some lettering, like cartoons and good illustrations, has become famous because of its style and design and is remembered long after the promotion is over. So there is room in all fields of commercial art to get to the top and have a success.

Make words do something for the artwork. Sometimes this is harder to do than drawing and sometimes the lettering takes over completely, as in this illustration from the Mecanorma catalogue.

Designers and Artists

I think we should consider for a moment or two the role of these two groups of people, who are working in very similar fields and indeed sometimes on the same job as each other. Although these two groups may be working on the same contract, they may never actually be in touch with each other, and yet what the one does will very much affect the work of the other.

Sometimes a designer will be commissioned to draft out some alternative schemes for a customer to consider. The customer will continue to discuss the project with the designer, making all the changes and improvements they think are necessary until it is agreed. This is the stage when it is usually passed to an artist (or a signwriter) to produce the product in accordance with the designer's layout. Of course this is not always the case, but it is a common procedure and is normally the way agencies work – they do the negotiation with their client and prepare the rough and then commission the artist.

This is the advertising agency's rough design for the signboards on display at the entrance to Wilton House.

As with books and literary agents, so it is with artwork and art agents; they will add a percentage onto your work when they receive it from you, and pass it on to their client. There will be a slight difference in attitude on your part in this case as opposed to the previous time we mentioned agencies because here the agent has come to you in the first instance, which gives you a slightly better command over your fee. Therefore don't sell your work too cheaply, and make quite sure of what you are accepting from a design studio or agency because you don't want to have to deviate from the layout in any way if you can help it. If you do find it necessary to make alterations (and you may) then you must contact them before doing so. There are two good reasons for this: the first is that if you do not produce the work precisely in accordance with instructions, the client may well be unhappy and the designer/agent will be reluctant to pay you; the second reason is that if you should find it impossible to stick to the design, either because of wrong scaling or poor proportions etc in the layout, then you may well be justified in adding a percentage to your own bill for the inconvenience it has caused you.

This is a design for a book jacket. Obviously it is a rough only – but the difficulty generally is to know how to interpret the finished artwork. If you put in too much detail, or if you work it up too meticulously, the designer may think you have lost the 'feel' he wanted. Hence it is essential to ask the questions first that will ensure you don't make that mistake.

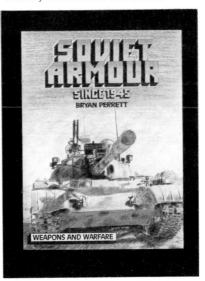

Consultation with all interested parties can never be overdone I find. Sometimes when I add up all the time I have spent discussing a project with a customer it seems as if it will be impossible to charge for it. In fact, the more involved discussion there is in preparing the groundwork, the less time is spent in experimenting on paper – so it balances itself out in the end.

Get it right with your client or agent.

It may be a thought when you are having your own stationery printed that you include the word 'designer', as this will widen your scope considerably and give you the chance to charge an 'origination' fee. I think I should make it clearly understood that some people are designers and as such could not themselves produce a finished piece of work to a good standard. Equally there are those who are excellent practitioners in the field of finished artwork and lettering, always provided they have been given a layout to work to. There are of course those who can do both!

A few examples of some of the words used on business cards and letterheads.

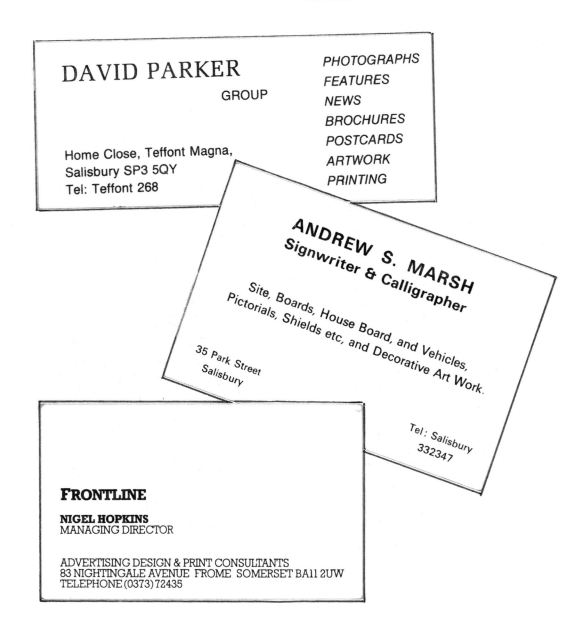

ROBIN HEATING SERVICES

CENTRAL HEATING CONTRACTORS

DOUBLE GLAZING CONSULTANTS

147 REDDITCH ROAD
EVESHAM
WORCESTERSHIRE
PHONE 6931 (4 LINES)

Eileen M. Divine
Creative Services

5334 Rue de Ville
Indianapolis, Indiana 46220
(317) 259-4860

divinedesign

Our Gang STUDIOS ®

'Contractors', 'Consultants', 'Creative Services' and 'Studios' are
all good words to include in your letterheads.

The question of colour matching and understanding between everyone concerned has to be somehow communicated, and clearly a system of colour matching and numbering must be used; luckily there are two generally accepted systems in use for just this purpose. One is the British Standard Institute's system (used mainly in the paint trade) where a paint carrying a BSI number will match another product carrying the same number. The other system, which is in more general use in the studio, is called the Pantone system. Again it relies on close matching of identical numbers so that they can be quoted and referred to in the Pantone colour swatches in the studio. This system of colour matching and choosing is extended to cover markers (so that you can actually use the specified colours in your layout) and sheets of colour/tint overlays, all using the same numbering system, which incidentally covers over 500 colours.

Colour markers come in many sizes and with a selection of 'points'. Remember, some are permanent and some are fugitive; some are light fast and some are not.

Get into the habit of using a recognised system like this — it gives you peace of mind to know that you have given a professional specification which cannot later be the subject of some sort of wrangle if colours don't match.

Keeping Records

Your studio will soon begin to look busy; you will accumulate bits of paper so fast that you will be amazed, and your desk, chairs and all flat surfaces will be the home (temporary of course) for just about everything from trivial doodles to important artwork. Studios are always like that and, because they are, I would like to make a strong recommendation that a 'loose method' for keeping such bits and pieces be adopted, otherwise the situation will get out of control and you will spend more and more time searching for 'lost' paperwork.

All that is necessary is something simple and adaptable. As you can see you will acquire pieces of paper in all shapes and sizes – perhaps a separate clip for the small pieces might be a good idea because they do tend to get a bit lost among the big bits.

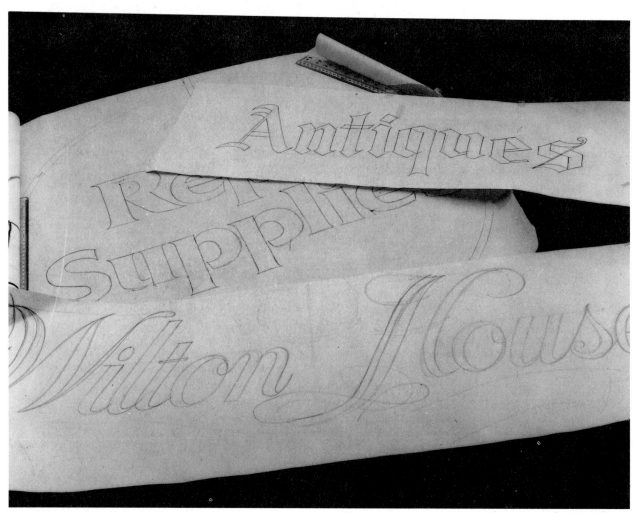

You can imagine just how important it is to keep these tracings. Some of them will be used over and over again and will save you many hours of work.

The space taken up in your studio by your records and details is probably giving the best return on your money that you are likely to get.

WELCOME TO
Wilton House
THE HOME OF THE EARL OF PEMBROKE

ADVENTURE
PLAYGROUND

FREE CAR &
COACH PARKS

LICENSED
RESTAURANT

MODEL
SOLDIERS

DOLLS
HOUSES

MODEL
RAILWAY

OPENING TIMES
Tues - Sat & Bank Holidays. 11am - 6pm
Sundays, 1pm - 6pm
Last admission to the House 5.15pm

OPENING DATES
Open to the Public from early March/April
to early October

The finished sign situated outside Wilton House, showing the end
product from some of the tracings on the previous page.

As time goes by and you become established, you will eventually begin to get repeat jobs; work you did for the first time some months ago – maybe even years ago. When you did it originally you probably spent some time in drawing up the logo from a sample letterhead to about 30 in (75 cm) high for use in a window display, or something equally time-consuming. The question is – did you keep a drawing or tracing of it, and what did you do with it if you did? If you did not keep a record (a tracing is always the most useful record as it can be put to so many uses) you will find yourself doing it all again, which will be a great shame. But, assuming you did keep a copy, I hope it is not going to be one of those bits of paper that litter the studio. This is where I suggest the loose method is used by fixing a few hooks under a shelf or along the wall in an out-of-the-way place so that your papers, copy, tracings etc can be bulldogged on to them. Remember, some of these papers will be quite large, too large to be put into drawers for instance, and so to hang them in this way is

ideal because it keeps them flat and you can see at a glance what you have on the clip. I may say that some of my templates and logos have been used so often that my ballpoint has nearly cut through the paper, but it has saved me hours of work.

I would also like to stress the need to keep a record of the prices you charge, and the date. This will serve as a convenient guide when working out new charges or if you get that repeat order; all you will need to do is uprate the old bill by the usual percentage increase.

The other record that is so necessary is measurement. It is very common to receive a telephone call asking for a repeat of a job you did some time ago which has become lost or destroyed. Nobody at the customer's end seems to know very much about it – they just hope you will have all the details and can produce another. So if you have kept a tracing, and the measurements, you can most likely go straight into the job without any fuss and be generally very professional about the whole thing.

10 AIRBRUSHING

An airbrush is a piece of equipment that does a superb job in a way that nothing else can. It is an expensive piece of equipment that requires a certain amount of care and meticulous attention to its cleaning. In essence it is a highly-developed paint spray mainly for use in the studio, but as there is now such a wide variety of models it means the range of use has become that much wider, giving the airbrush artist unlimited scope for his talents.

Although an airbrush is not an essential piece of the commercial artist's equipment, it does make a difference to the jobs you do and the way you do them; in fact an artist can easily become hooked on airbrushing, and some become specialists in the field earning their living as airbrush artists – for which skilful work substantial fees can be charged.

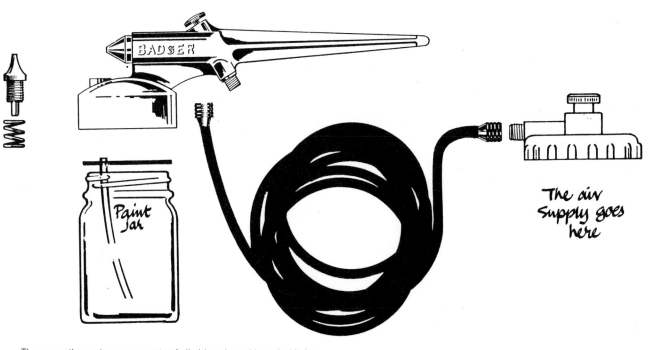

These are the main components of all airbrushes although this is a very basic one to start with.

Everybody is well acquainted with the classic look of airbrush work – that super-smooth, even-graded, flawless layer of colour, where the purity of it can sometimes cause you to wonder if it is really paint or some photographic process. Actually, airbrushing is not all like that; it is also capable of a more varied use, such as splatter effects of varying courseness, fine lines (against a straight edge), mechanical curves (against a flexi-curve or standard French curves) and intricate artwork with the use of masks, to say nothing of freehand work on landscapes, figures, portraits and skies. There is no limit to the level of prowess that can be achieved; it is only governed by the artist's ingenuity and skill, with patience playing a large part in the success of the work, since a lot of time must be devoted to the preparation of the paint and the maintenance of the brush itself. Perhaps the most time of all is spent on cutting and laying the masks; or even the precise layout of the drawing in the first place for the masks to be cut from. This is a perfect illustration of the golden rule – 'no hurry, no worry'.

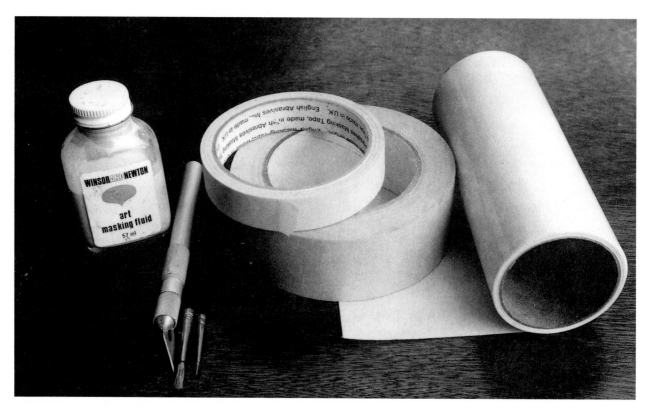

The items above are enough to get you started. Ordinary paper masking tape for masking round the artwork edges, for a nice straight and tidy finish. Liquid mask for the more intricate shapes to be used with a brush, and masking film. This latter is the most extensively used, but make sure your stencil knife is really sharp.

As the opportunities for the airbrush are so far-reaching, it is unlikely (although by no means impossible) that the artist will on his own cover all aspects from detailed mechanical illustrations to vehicle decoration, but if he should then he will need more than one airbrush.

Although there are technically two types of airbrush, there are actually four broad areas of work where it can be used.

1) Illustration (mainly mechanical and technical subjects).
2) Vehicle decoration (therefore mainly used in workshops).
3) Colouring three-dimensional models (as a hobbyist or professional model maker).
4) Freehand extension to the more traditional methods of painting.

This is one of the most popular uses of the airbrush – all mechanical and 'hard surface' subjects come out well.

Types of Airbrush

The two main types are the single-action lever and the double-action lever. As the name would suggest, the single-action is the simplest of the two, and as might be expected has a limited use. The single-action lever refers to the control the artist has over the paint/air proportion, which in this case is nil; the paint and air are in fixed ratio to each other. That makes this type of brush not suitable for precision work on a small scale such as book illustration or photographic retouching. It is, however, excellent for background work, i.e. taking out the confusing backgrounds in photographs and for shading in large areas. It is very good also for spraying models and all small-scale painting jobs, and the right one for personalising T-shirts either freehand or through a stencil. The advantage of this brush is its simple maintenance; providing you finish up each time with a good spraying through with thinners (or water, depending on what paint you have been using) and then a good blow through with air, you will not need to do anything more before you use it next time.

The artist is beginning work here on a portrait. The picture clearly shows the pencilled outline, the masking film (in yellow here to show up more clearly) and a double action airbrush.

For precision work, other than just blocking in with flat colour, the artist will need the double-action lever brush. There are a number of makes and models readily available and all adopt the same principle; the control button is pressed down to release the air (the further down, the more air) and the same lever is also pulled back to release the paint (the further back, the more paint). This gives the artist infinite control over the air/paint ratio, enabling him to express himself to the maximum.

There are also air erasers which look and operate like an airbrush but spray an abrasive from their reservoirs instead of paint. They will remove paint and ink without smudging and can be used to blend highlights and soften shadows; they can also be used as an etching tool for working on glass.

For work on a larger scale, such as displays at exhibitions, murals, and artwork on vehicles, a larger type of airbrush is needed – more on the lines of a spray gun where there is a larger reservoir and larger nozzle.

The illustration here represents all that is best in a double action system. This type of airbrush has been on the market for many years and has always been a favourite among professionals.

Having made your choice of airbrush, you now have to decide on your air supply which on average must provide approximately 30 psi (2 kg per sq. cm). Your choice will be between an aerosol can (for small jobs), an air cylinder (such as divers use), a compressor, and a motor car spare wheel! You now have to ask yourself the difficult question – How much airbrushing will you be doing? Since you are working for a profit, if you are not sure how much of your work is going to be with an airbrush it may not be sensible at this stage to invest in a compressor (which is the best air supply), because as with most things the best is the most expensive, therefore one of the alternatives might be the answer.

The air cylinder is the best alternative and is cheap to refill; it will see you through a lot of work too and stands quite snugly at the side of the drawing board. The aerosol can, on the other hand, is extremely handy and ideal for small jobs such as retouching photographs and highlighting or shading. For lengthy periods of use, however, the aerosol can would have to be replaced often and would become expensive. The last alternative is the car spare wheel. This is naturally the cheapest way of obtaining your air supply, and it works perfectly well providing you accept the drawbacks, among which are its bulk and its weight. Naturally you have to have a footpump on hand as well to maintain the pressure, but apart from that it is a good standby system, although the pressure is inclined to drop rather quickly and must be maintained at about 30 psi, otherwise the paint will not atomise properly and will begin to splatter. You will incidentally need an adaptor to the standard air line in order to use it with a spare wheel, but they are very cheap and easily available.

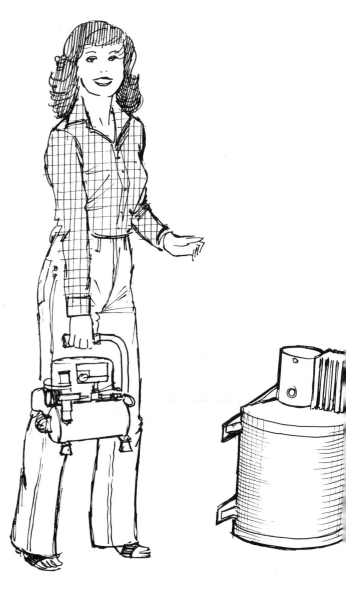

Aerosol cans of propellant come in various sizes...a stand-by alternative is the spare wheel.

There are many types of compressor and as you can see, they are not at all bulky or difficult to handle.

Masks

A large percentage of airbrush work is used in conjunction with a 'mask', the object of which is to confine the effect of the airbrush to a particular area. To do this there are two types of mask – film and liquid. Liquid mask is a latex-based medium, sold in small jars for use by all artists, not just in connection with airbrushing. It is painted on the area to be masked with a brush (which must be washed in warm water immediately after use) and left to dry. The painting is then completed, and when dry the liquid mask can easily be removed by rubbing gently with a finger, leaving the area untouched by paint.

A film mask has to be cut to shape with a stencil knife. This is sold as a transparent film in sheet or roll form and has a low-tack adhesive backing. The shape to be masked is cut roughly and slightly oversize from the film, and the protective backing is removed. It is then laid in position on the artwork and cut accurately to shape with a stencil knife, using very little pressure; the excess film is then peeled away and the work is ready for airbrushing. This aspect of the work does need practice but you will soon learn the tricks of the trade and develop your own knacks for dealing with particular problems. It is in fact the practice and subsequent skill that goes into this that is largely responsible for the success the artist achieves at the end of the day. Sometimes as many as twenty or thirty masks will be used in one piece of work, meaning that the masking time far exceeds the brushing time.

Airbrush inks are of a very high quality and come in a range of good bright colours.

The spare tyre adaptor is screwed directly onto the tyre valve – it has to be taken off to re-inflate the tyre when the pressure drops below the working level.

Inks

Special attention must be paid to the ink or paint you use. Although it is true that almost any ink or paint can be used provided it is fed at the right consistency (which should never be thicker than milk), nevertheless experience will show that some inks/paints are in general more suitable than others and also that some are better than others for a particular job.

I seem to remember saying earlier that 'the work is done in the head before you start', and it is very true here. Before setting up your equipment you should have a careful look at the job to work out the sequence of colours and masks in your head. Try to visualise yourself actually doing the job and imagine the paint going on the paper. In this way you can generally decide which type of paint to use to arrive quickly at the result you want. Some paints will get you there quicker than others – for instance if you are doing a simple background job on a photograph, gouache will get rid of the unwanted area in one or two coats because it has great opacity, whereas you would use watercolour or ink on the subtle remodelling of a portrait.

There is another way your head has to programme the work for you, which is the way the colour is to be laid down. To take a very simple example, if you have to make a number of white stars on a night sky, you have to decide whether it will be best in the circumstances to put white gouache stars directly onto a Prussian blue night sky by cutting them out of a mask, or whether it is better to put the stars in first with masking fluid on the white paper and then spray the night sky all over, rubbing off the masking when the sky is dry and leaving the stars as white paper. Your decision would undoubtedly depend on other considerations at the time as well, such as the size and shape of the stars, and (as yours will be a practical studio) whether your masking fluid has dried up!

Exercises

If airbrushing is going to be a new departure for you, you should have fun and do some exercises with the airbrush to get used to the materials and handling the equipment. It even needs practice in the simple things like filling the reservoir, or keeping the airline from knocking over pots of paint, and even in just laying down the airbrush without spilling the paint from the reservoir. You will soon start getting results that please you, providing you stick to the golden rule and don't hurry to get something finished.

There are some almost standard exercises which cover the types of surface and shapes you will eventually be trying to express, i.e. cones, balls, cubes and flat areas. Just to make your exercises more interesting, try turning them into tennis and cricket balls, dice and dunces' caps. When you get tired of these try a slightly more complicated version – perhaps a corrugated sheet.

A good way to practise cutting masks is to first cut out one or two diagrams or drawings from a magazine, and try cutting masks for them. Airbrush them in with watercolour or ink so that the lines are not obliterated and you will be agreeably surprised when you see how good they look. One point to watch out for is that all airbrush artists have to handle their work a lot; it is therefore essential to keep your hands clean and free from grease, as one greasy fingerprint is enough to spoil your work. If you are working in acrylic or other waterproof materials, on a long job you can occasionally wash it over to remove any greasiness, but in the case of watercolour of course you can't do that. It would therefore be a good idea to keep the area you are not actually working on covered with a sheet of paper or card, just to be on the safe side.

You should try freehand use of the airbrush as well; it is strange but it is often forgotten that there is great potential in this sort of use. Imaginative cloud effects are not only easy but very exciting, especially if you change the colour quickly, using wet on wet, letting the colours blend of their own accord. Likewise rays of sunlight coming through the trees or through a break in the clouds can be created in a few seconds and look very convincing. Among other interesting subjects for experiment are haloes, explosions, speed lines on moving objects, and out-of-focus backgrounds. Vignetting, too, is a freehand skill that is useful to acquire and does need practice to produce a good even fade. Don't just stick to conventional work, break new ground and try things for yourself; you will be surprised what you can do.

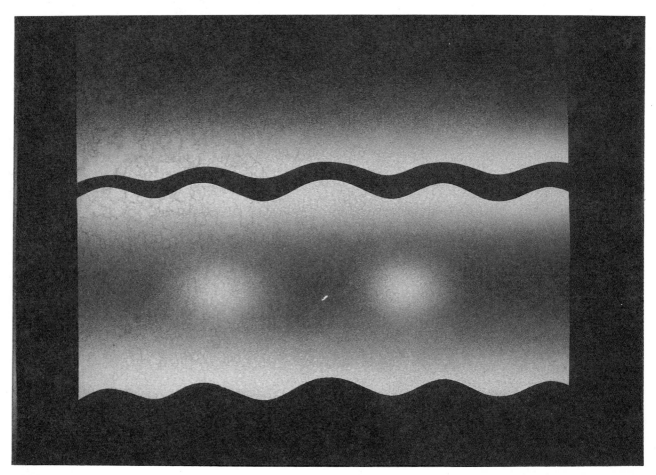

11 LETTERING

People who do lettering are referred to as 'writers'. There are two sorts of writers, 'poster' and 'sign', and you will find they are considered to be two quite different professions because the approach, equipment and style of each are not at all alike. There are some first-class signwriters who make only mediocre poster writers and conversely some very good poster writers will not even attempt to write a sign.

Posters

Poster writing differs from signwriting in many ways but mainly in its position while it is being written; posters are written with the paper resting flat on the bench, and signs are written vertically.

Posters are sometimes required in quite large sizes, for instance pelmets, banners and streamers which can be as much as 30 ft (9 m) or so, so you will need a good long bench on these occasions, otherwise it will have to be the floor.

Under normal circumstances you will first need to mark out your poster, which usually means running some pencil lines across the poster as a guide for the tops and bottoms of the letters. To do this quickly, first make sure the bottom edge of your paper is level with the front edge of the bench, then with your mahl stick in your left hand and a pencil in your right hand, and holding them as shown, you can make all the lines you need without any measurements and at great speed.

A useful tip here is that if you are working on fluorescent paper you will find it is very difficult to remove the pencil marks when you have finished with them, as it always leaves an ugly 'rub' mark behind. So, to avoid this, use the wrong end of an artist's or signwriter's brush to score a mark in the surface which afterwards does not need to be removed.

Use the 'wrong end' of a brush to mask out guide lines on fluorescent paper. When the lettering has been added, the bruised lines won't show.

Quick FAST ELEGANT Informal FREE !

Think of the meaning of the words you are writing and try to make a graphic interpretation of that meaning. This is what makes a poster/leaflet/sign interesting. It also makes them interesting to do!

Poster writing requires a much thinner paint than signwriting, and because of this the letters are formed in a much freer and quicker way, with the result that they take on a great deal of character. However, posters being what they are, i.e. a fairly short-lived requirement, the price that can be charged for them has to be modest, so speed and style are the key words. This means the characters are not 'blocked' or built up but are achieved by using a selection of 'one-stroke' brushes, or similar, which enable you to make the letters at a stroke.

All poster writers have a few carefully-chosen alphabets which they use for the majority of the time, and the combination of which when used skilfully produces an interesting and eye-catching poster. These alphabets will probably have been developed personally by the writer and so will have taken on an individuality of a freestyle nature.

For posters you should avoid the excessive use of 'squared-off' letters, or letters with serifs or any other complicated form. Once you have got one or two styles at your fingertips it only remains to practise and develop them in an eye-catching and legible way.

In the same way that writers keep one or two pet alphabets in their head, they also keep a few standard layouts there too. These have been arrived at by a combination of experience and diligent observation. A good poster should have a bit of 'weight' about it somewhere; perhaps a reverse panel or some flashes or even one or two chunky words. It doesn't matter how you provide the weight, just so long as you do; there is nothing more boring and amateurish than a poster that looks as if it has been typeset by a printer. Your aim should be to make your poster as different to a printed poster as you can, which means not only must your lettering be more free and easy, but you must try to get away from working in straight lines. It will never look attractive or have any design quality if all your lettering goes from left to right straight across the page. Form them into groups; put some on a diagonal or in a curve; make some wavy, even make some totter and tumble – but NEVER put one letter under another in a vertical fashion. This is where the poster writer scores so heavily because it costs him nothing to get some variation and individuality into his work, whereas to a printer this can be a nightmare.

You must be able to do a poster quickly, at the same time getting the priorities in the right order. Remember to make sure you do them the right way – landscape or portrait.

144

PORTRAIT

The same will apply to the colours you use. It costs no more to use three colours than it does to use one, and yet see how much more it looks worth. If you are working on fluorescent paper, the colours you can use will be much more restricted – in fact it is customary to use only black as this produces a very strong visual combination. It always pays to use waterproof colours even if they are not destined to be used outside, because they are often placed inside a window where there is condensation, and it is surprising how frequently a poster comes into contact with damp hands or a humid atmosphere.

Take into account the paper sizes too before you start; not that it makes any difference to you what size you work at, but it will make a great deal of difference if they are to be printed in any quantity. On the subject of size, make sure that everyone is clear about which way round the poster is to go – landscape or portrait.

The brushes you need must be long-haired (preferably sable), and can be either standard signwriting brushes or one-stroke. Whichever you choose, the paint is used very thin and the brush should be fully loaded as in watercolour painting. If you are writing a number of posters, don't try to complete each poster at a time; it is better to do a selected part of each one in turn on a mass-production basis, i.e. if you are doing twelve posters, do the top line of each of the twelve before you start the next bit. This way your lettering will adopt a 'swing', and the finished posters will have a rhythm which is difficult to get if you keep doing little bits of lettering to complete each poster in turn.

LANDSCAPE

Some poster artists like to pencil out a master copy first and then, by using a light-box or a window, they trace through the layout on to each poster proper, ready for painting. There are some advantages to this method – one is that there is no need for any pencilled guide lines for the top and bottom edges of the lettering (so it saves time on the rubbing out afterwards); another advantage is that there is no measuring needed, in fact if you do the tracing through carefully enough you will not need to do any cleaning up at all. You never want to do any more cleaning up than is absolutely necessary, because not only does it take time but also, unless the lettering has had plenty of time to dry thoroughly, the rubbing out of the guide lines can smudge or disfigure it if you are not very careful, and to correct smudged lettering so that it doesn't show can be very difficult and time-consuming, and also rarely totally successful.

A window makes a good light-box for posters and other large-scale work.

So far I have assumed that the lettering is for handwritten posters. If it is for subsequently printed posters then the lettering becomes artwork and can be corrected and altered until it is right. This would allay the great fear of all writers, that is lack of concentration, which inevitably leads to a spelling mistake or a missing word or letter. In the case of handwritten posters, this is one ruined; if it is artwork, on the other hand, it can be corrected without difficulty.

Whatever types and styles you have selected to use, among them should be a 'script'. It is very seldom that you can avoid using a script of some sort for very long, as it is most useful for setting off or relieving an otherwise dull layout. There are so many script faces which have become standards that it should not be very difficult to choose one for your collection.

Small-scale work, such as menus, testimonials, certificates etc, is normally done with a pen, although I hasten to add not always. Most manufacturers make a whole range of pens for the professional, both dip and fill. The important thing is to use the right pen for the job (as with brushes); you will not be able to perform properly without the right tool. So decide what sort of lettering you are going to use: copperplate, italic, roman or plain freestyle handwritten – there are pens for all of them.

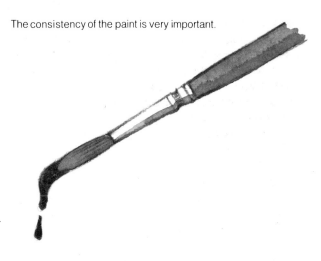

The consistency of the paint is very important.

The paint needs to be thin and the brush must be very good tempered. Get a good 'flow' going and don't try to work at a word – it must be done without hesitation and without going back over any of it.

Distinction

Summer Sale Big Event

Enormous Bargains

Main Course

Signs and Signwriting

Signwriting and the preparation of signs need more room and a bit more equipment than posters. It also needs more care in the process of forming the letters and the whole performance takes longer to complete, due mainly to the nature of the paint, which being thicker takes longer to cover the same amount of ground, and also takes longer to dry, usually two or three hours instead of the half-hour in posters. Because signs are more permanent items than posters it is natural to expect to devote more time to them for that reason alone, despite the fact that the wordage might be just the same.

Be careful to choose good lettering, even from a catalogue and then be precise about the way you enlarge it. Remember, all the imperfections in signwriting show up most at a distance.

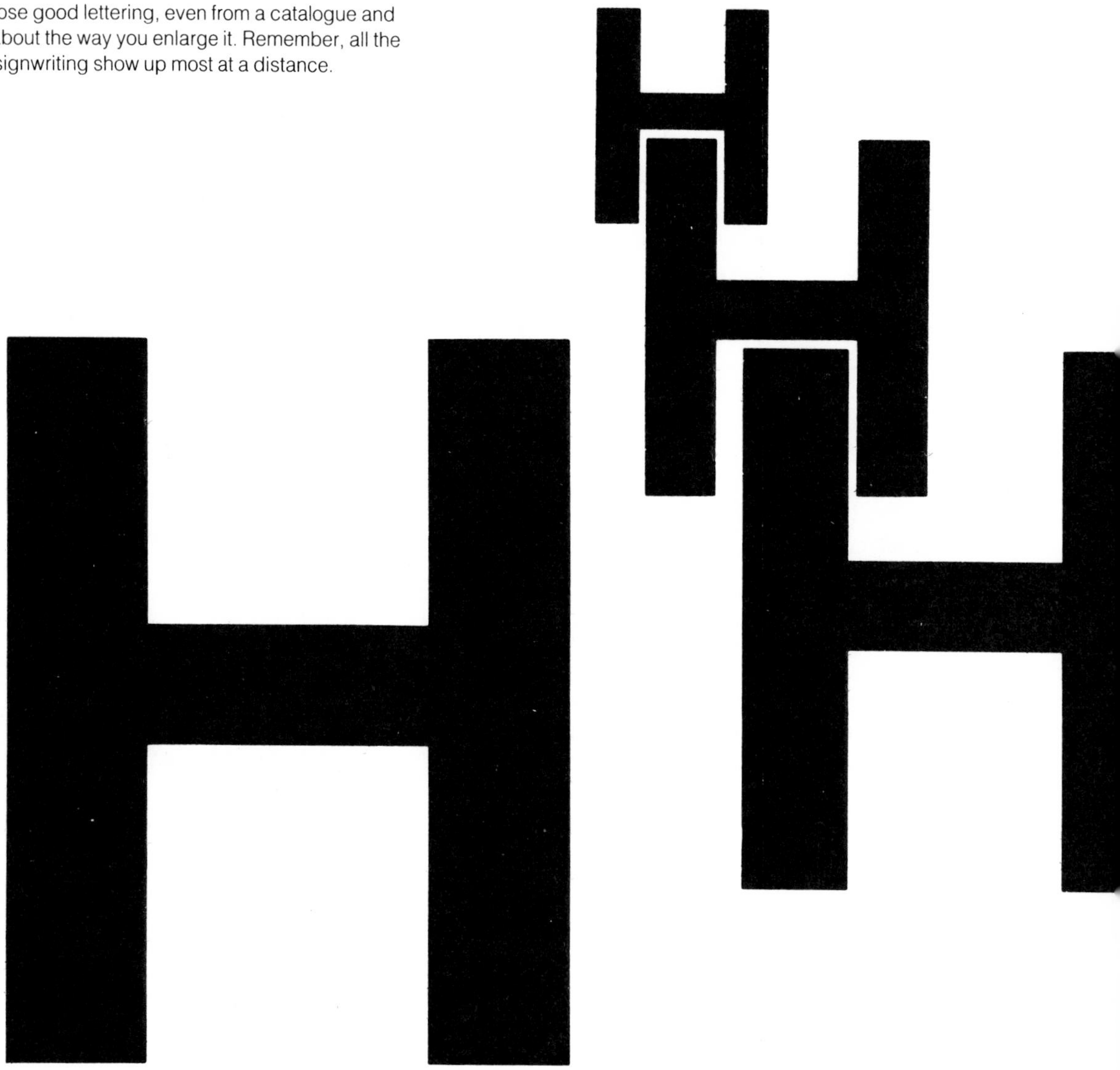

ABCDEFGHIJKL
MNOPQRSTUVWXY
ÆŒ1234567890
abcdefghijklmnop
qrstuvwxyzæœ

In order to produce good lettering you must start with a good, well-prepared surface, that is one that is smooth (not necessarily glossy) and without blemishes, like unfilled grain or orange-peel paintwork – and it must be dry. Modern paints have a disturbing way of feeling dry when they are not actually chemically dry, which means that if you work on them the new lettering will soften the surface and eventually dry with wrinkles. It is always ideal if you can leave a painted surface at least overnight before you start to letter it.

It is essential that you have the right tools and materials handy before you begin. You will need your signwriting brushes (the sizes will depend on the lettering) and writing enamel in the correct colour. You will want your mahl stick, a chinagraph pencil, turpentine or white spirit, a piece of rag and a long ruler. If you are using my earlier suggestion for a mahl stick then you will not want the ruler.

You can also make use of low-tack masking tape to help you keep the tops and bottoms of your letters sharp and straight; most signwriters use it these days although there are some types of letter where there is no advantage in using it. Low-tack tape is also indispensable for masking round large areas to be filled in with paint or for making really straight and sharp lines and borders. It does actually speed up the writing time on ordinary block lettering.

In all trades and professions there are skills to be practised, and we now arrive at one which is fundamental to the writer. It refers to the holding and manipulation of the brush, which in poster writing can be held any way it happens to suit you, as if you were holding a pen or pencil and the lettering were formed with it being thus held. This is not so in signwriting however; the brush must be held so that it can be twisted between the fingers whenever a curve is attempted, otherwise the chisel end of the brush will produce a thick and thin stroke round the curve and it would be extremely difficult to produce a perfect shape using a brush this way. By twisting it as the curve is made, and keeping the flat of the brush edge on the curve, it helps the writer to make the shape with considerable assurance. The twisting of the brush between the fingers does, however, need some practice.

Peel off the tape to leave a nice sharp edge.

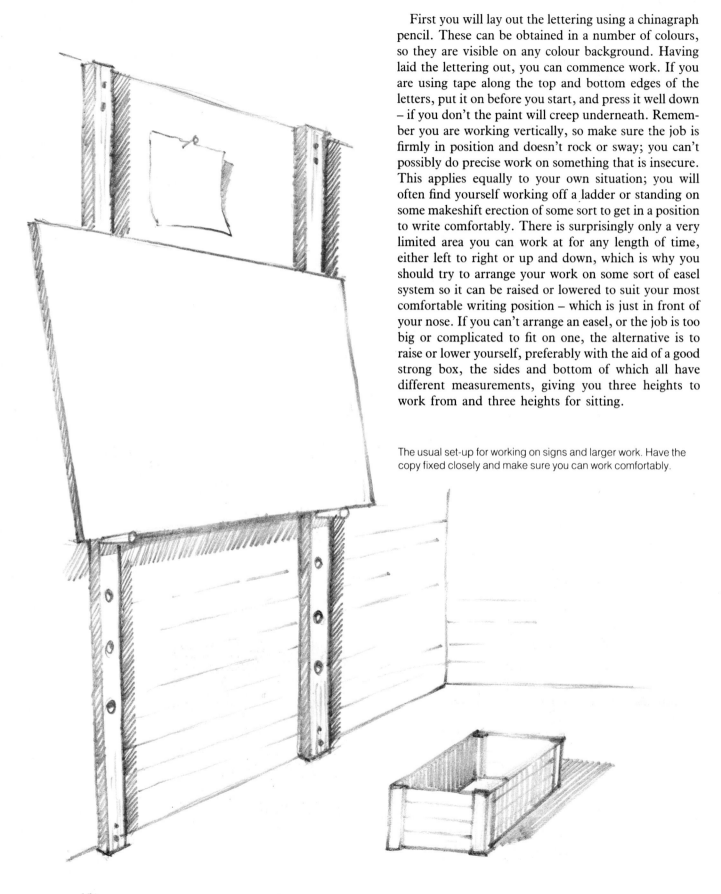

First you will lay out the lettering using a chinagraph pencil. These can be obtained in a number of colours, so they are visible on any colour background. Having laid the lettering out, you can commence work. If you are using tape along the top and bottom edges of the letters, put it on before you start, and press it well down – if you don't the paint will creep underneath. Remember you are working vertically, so make sure the job is firmly in position and doesn't rock or sway; you can't possibly do precise work on something that is insecure. This applies equally to your own situation; you will often find yourself working off a ladder or standing on some makeshift erection of some sort to get in a position to write comfortably. There is surprisingly only a very limited area you can work at for any length of time, either left to right or up and down, which is why you should try to arrange your work on some sort of easel system so it can be raised or lowered to suit your most comfortable writing position – which is just in front of your nose. If you can't arrange an easel, or the job is too big or complicated to fit on one, the alternative is to raise or lower yourself, preferably with the aid of a good strong box, the sides and bottom of which all have different measurements, giving you three heights to work from and three heights for sitting.

The usual set-up for working on signs and larger work. Have the copy fixed closely and make sure you can work comfortably.

Styles

The style of letter you use will not be the same as in poster work because the signwriting enamel will not allow it. I have already mentioned that it is thicker and so you must work slower, which means some of the freedom is lost; the characters need more building up, and since you are working upright you will not be able to flood the paint on as you did with posters, with the consequence that even the application of the paint must be considered as it will be necessary to apply it with care, and in the case of large lettering brush it out. Since most signwriting is done with a gloss, any uneven brushwork will show when it catches the light.

The letters for signwriting are formed with more care and are more elaborate or at least precise. Generally speaking these lettering styles are more orthodox.

To start with don't try to be all things to all men. Choose a few alphabets that you like the look of and use them until you know them off by heart and you don't need to be continually referring to the catalogue. You will find that some standard typefaces need to be 'boldened up' for signs and displays; elegant styles are all very nice but they do tend to get a bit lost when in competition with other visual images.

Paints

There are proper signwriting paints (mainly enamels) available and you should try to use them, although they may not be available locally. Send for a list of all products for signwriters (see the end of the book) and you will find there is a special paint for most types of work. The main property of signwriting enamel is its opacity, its ability to cover in one coat in most cases, although with some colours a second coat is necessary. Also available are tubes of intense colour which can be used on their own, or added to enamel to give it greater opacity and intensity of colour.

Ha1

If the thin strokes are too thin they can't be seen from a distance and the words become meaningless making the letters bolder improves legibility.

Ha1

Keep your signwriting enamels together in an old box or drawer. Have a handle at the top so you can carry it about without upsetting the paints. This way you can even carry jars of thinners or white spirit quite safely.

SYNTHETIC WRITING ENAMELS

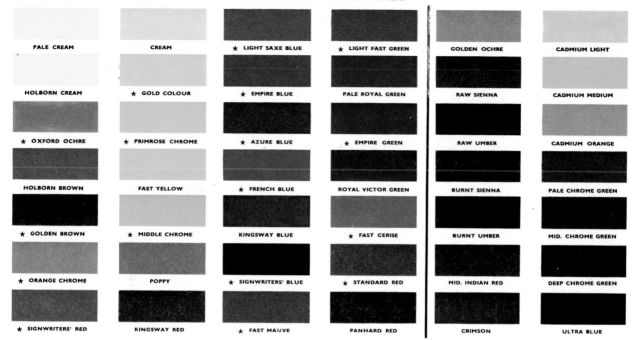

PALE CREAM	CREAM	★ LIGHT SAXE BLUE	★ LIGHT FAST GREEN	GOLDEN OCHRE	CADMIUM LIGHT
HOLBORN CREAM	★ GOLD COLOUR	★ EMPIRE BLUE	PALE ROYAL GREEN	RAW SIENNA	CADMIUM MEDIUM
★ OXFORD OCHRE	★ PRIMROSE CHROME	★ AZURE BLUE	★ EMPIRE GREEN	RAW UMBER	CADMIUM ORANGE
HOLBORN BROWN	FAST YELLOW	★ FRENCH BLUE	ROYAL VICTOR GREEN	BURNT SIENNA	PALE CHROME GREEN
★ GOLDEN BROWN	★ MIDDLE CHROME	KINGSWAY BLUE	★ FAST CERISE	BURNT UMBER	MID. CHROME GREEN
★ ORANGE CHROME	POPPY	★ SIGNWRITERS' BLUE	★ STANDARD RED	MID. INDIAN RED	DEEP CHROME GREEN
★ SIGNWRITERS' RED	KINGSWAY RED	★ FAST MAUVE	PANHARD RED	CRIMSON	ULTRA BLUE

Don't try working with anything other than paint/enamel and brushes. Writing enamels are bright in colour and have excellent covering ability. Most of them will cover in one coat.

Tubes of intense colour can be added to most paints to improve their covering power and their brilliance. This makes them a must for the busy writer.

Gold Leaf

The only truly satisfactory way to produce gold lettering is still with gold leaf. Unfortunately it is rather a slow operation, and this coupled with the price of leaf makes it an expensive job. It is clearly not the way to approach any run-of-the-mill work, and if you do use gold leaf make sure the customer knows what he is getting. Gold or silver leaf comes in small books and is obtainable as 'loose leaf' or 'transfer leaf'. Loose leaf is what you use when you mirror-gild the inside of a window, such as the traditional solicitors or accountants. Transfer leaf is much easier to use and is what you will need if you are surface gilding your lettering, also if you wish to re-gild a picture frame or candlestick.

Cleaning Brushes

If you are using your brush continuously over a long period of time you will find the paint begins to dry up where the hair meets the ferrule, and later on in the centre of the brush itself. To avoid this happening try keeping a small jar of thinners handy so you can occasionally give the brush a swirl round to keep the brush soft. Whenever you break off from writing, either for coffee or lunch or even overnight, don't bother to wash out your brush each time, in fact busy writers never wash them out; they are left in a dish of solvent or cleaner (not to be confused with thinners) and in this way they will remain soft and ready for use. Whatever you do, don't stand them upright, as the hairs will become bent in only a few minutes, and then they will be useless for writing until you have straightened them again. Just lay them in a tin lid or in a jar that has been lodged at an angle. Brushes can stay for weeks like this without any ill effects.

After you have been using a brush for some time, it helps to give it a few minutes in a brush cleaner. This dissolves the paint that is beginning to dry up at the base of the ferrule.

Both of these methods work equally well and can stay like this for long periods. There is a small advantage perhaps with the tin lid or saucer in that a number of brushes can be laid in the solvent in a radial fashion.

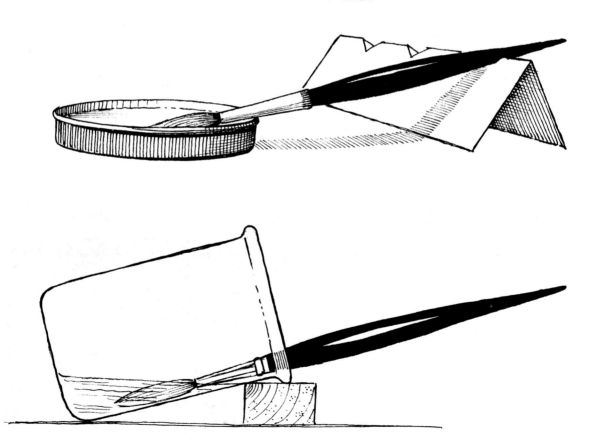

Glasswork

Windows present rather special problems. Most of the year they are very cold to work on and can easily cause your hands to ache and become numb. As can be imagined, the surface is sometimes difficult to see, which makes focusing on your pencil lines a real problem, although an effective way round that is to tape a sheet of paper on the other side of the glass to stop the confusing images behind and to give you a background while you are working. If you are lucky enough to be working on the inside, you will have to work back to front, of course, which is not altogether easy and is best overcome by drafting the work out first on paper and then taping it in position on the outside; from inside you can see your lines through the paper and can work directly from them. As it is most precarious to attempt any lettering back to front without some good guide lines, this solves that problem and also saves some time working on the cold window.

Another snag is that the paint doesn't adhere to the glass very successfully; it is inclined to run down from the bottom of the letters unless the paint is kept at exactly the right consistency. Because of this you will not be able to apply very much paint at a time and so it may need a second coat to produce a really dense colour. The tubes of intense colour are ideal for working on glass, and if you do your marking out with a red or yellow chinagraph pencil the chances of a successful outcome are greatly enhanced.

Writing on Vehicles

Putting the livery and lettering on vehicles can be very rewarding to a signwriter as it transforms a plain mass-produced article into an individual moving advertisement. The principles and procedures for writing are just the same as for other writing jobs, although it does have its own particular drawbacks because of the surfaces being generally curved or ridged and because of the many obstructions specially designed to frustrate signwriters, in the guise of petrol caps, air vents, hinges, door handles and mirrors.

Before you make a start (even before you pencil out) on a vehicle, new or old, give it a thorough rub over with detergent or methylated spirit to remove any grease or dirt that ordinary washing may not have removed.

Tape the layout onto the outside of the window and then 'fill in' with paint on the inside. Then take away the layout.

Before you start work on a vehicle it is essential to give it a good hard rub over with detergent or methylated spirits.

Tracing Down

When you have to repeat yourself (as in the case of vehicles where there are two identical sides, and sometimes the back as well) it may be worth making a paper layout first. You can do this in the comparative comfort of your studio, and you will spend less time in a noisy, cold and smelly garage, and the layout will ensure that you get both sides the same. As I mentioned earlier, you must keep the layout in case the customer buys another vehicle; he will, however, be expected to pay the same fee.

When you have drawn the layout, turn it over and scribble over the back of your lines with a chinagraph pencil so that it will transfer easily onto the smooth surface of the vehicle. I suggest you keep a worn-out ball-point pen for the purpose of pressing through; this way if you have to use it many times the layout will not become a mass of thick inky lines – you will be able to follow your original lines as accurately after the sixth impression as after the first. Sheet transfer paper can be bought commercially and is usually pure graphite, which works very well on most surfaces but not on vehicles. It does, however, come in various colours and lasts a long time.

If you want to make your own transfer paper it is best to use a thin layout or drafting paper. Rub over one side with chalk and then with a tightly screwed-up paper tissue continue the rubbing until most of the chalk is rubbed into the paper. When this is done, blow away the surplus dust and lightly wipe the remainder away with a duster. The paper is now ready for use and will continue to be workable for a long time.

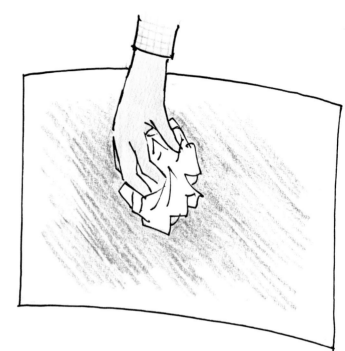

Scribble over the tracing paper with chalk or pastel and then rub it smooth with a screwed up paper tissue. Blow away the dust and it is ready for use.

Charging out your Work

The reason you are working is so that eventually you can charge a fee and so make a living. But often the method of calculating this fee is difficult to say the least. It is very easy for friends to tell you simply to work on a time and materials basis, but all of us who have to do it know it is not as easy as that. You have to take into account the times you make a mistake, or do it the wrong way so that it takes much longer, or the weather was so damp the paint wouldn't dry. These things make timing the job very difficult. Even materials are not easy to charge out since you very seldom buy in just what you need for the job. Apart from these complications there is the big one – how the finished job turns out; does it look worth what you feel you should charge for it? Or does it look better!

Clearly what you must do is calculate your time and materials as best you can and then take an objective view of the finished work. If it looks good and you think it will stand a little profit on top, then charge it – there is no sin in making a profit, and there will be plenty of times when you have to let your work go at bare cost anyway!

BIBLIOGRAPHY

Artist's Manual, Macdonald Educational 1980.

Ayres, James, *The Artist's Craft*, Phaidon 1985.

Dalley, Terence (Consultant Editor), *The Complete Guide to Illustration and Design*, Chartwell Books Inc. QED Publishing Ltd 1980.

Don Davy Manual of Drawing, Blandford Press 1986.

Hayes, Colin, *The Complete Guide to Painting and Drawing*, Phaidon 1979.

Laing, John (Consultant Editor), *Do It Yourself Graphic Design*, Ebury Press 1984.

Laing, John, and Saunders-Davies, Rhiannon, *Graphic Tools and Techniques*, Blandford Press 1986.

Smith, Stan, and Holt, Professor H.F. Ten (Editors), *The Illustrator's Handbook*, Macdonald Educational 1984.

INDEX